Light in a Spotless Mirror

FAITH AND SCHOLARSHIP
COLLOQUIES SERIES

Light in a Spotless Mirror

Reflections on Wisdom Traditions
in Judaism and Early Christianity

Edited by
James H. Charlesworth
and Michael A. Daise

Faith and Scholarship Colloquies

TRINITY PRESS INTERNATIONAL
A Continuum imprint
HARRISBURG • LONDON • NEW YORK

Trinity Press International, P.O. Box 1321, Harrisburg, PA 17105
Trinity Press International is a member of the
Continuum International Publishing Group.

Cover art: *A Conversation between Philosophers*, mosaic from Pompeii.
Museo Archeologico Nazionale, Naples, Italy.
Erich Lessing / Art Resource, NY.

Cover design: Wesley Hoke

Library of Congress Cataloging-in-Publication Data

Light in a spotless mirror : reflections on wisdom traditions in Judaism and
and early Christianity / edited by James H. Charlesworth and Michael A.
Daise.
    p. cm. – (Faith and scholarship colloquies)
    Includes bibliographical references (p.) and indexes.
    ISBN 1–56338–399–3
    1. Wisdom (Biblical personification) – Congresses. 2. Wisdom – Religious
aspects – Judaism – History of doctrines – Congresses. 3. Wisdom –
Religious aspects – Christianity – History of doctrines – Congresses.
I. Charlesworth, James H. II. Daise, Michael A. III. Series.
BS580.W58 L54 2003
223'.06 – dc21
                                           2002012929

Printed in the United States of America

03 04 05 06 07 08   10 9 8 7 6 5 4 3 2 1

Dedicated to
Dr. Joe Wesley Dickerson
and Irma Lou Wilcox
dedicated philanthropists
and fellow travelers

Contents

Contributors

PEDER BORGEN is Professor Emeritus of New Testament and Religion n the Greco-Roman World at the University of Trondheim in Norway.

JAMES H. CHARLESWORTH is George L. Collord Professor of New Testament Language and Literature and Director of the Dead Sea Scrolls project at Princeton Theological Seminary.

ROLAND MURPHY, O.Carm., was George Washington Ivey Professor of Old Testament, Emeritus, at Duke University.

PETER SCHÄFER is Perelman Professor of Jewish Studies and Professor of Religion at Princeton University and Director of the Institut für Judaistik at the Freie Universität in Berlin.

D. MOODY SMITH is George Washington Ivey Professor of New Testament, Emeritus, at Duke University.

Series Description

Faith and Scholarship Colloquies

This series explores the boundaries where faith and academic study intersect. At these borders, the sharp edge of current biblical scholarship is allowed to cut theologically and pose its often challenging questions for traditional faith. The series includes contributions from leading scholars in contemporary biblical studies. As Christian faith seeks to send a word on target in our day, as powerful as those in the past, it needs to sharpen its perception and proclamation from honest and truthful insights in human knowledge, from first-century archaeology to modern linguistics.

Introduction

Wisdom, a Spotless Mirror, and Reflections of Traditions

James H. Charlesworth

> For she is a reflection of eternal light,
> a spotless mirror of the working of God,
> and an image of his goodness.
> — Wisdom of Solomon 7:26, NRSV

After Alexander the Great's death in 323 B.C.E., Jews more directly pondered questions that have intermittently bothered each of us. These gifted and highly trained scholars, especially in Jerusalem and Alexandria, turned increasingly to reflections on the eternal questions that define those who reflect on human life.

Some of these Jewish sages asked how God created the universe. The question is as old as our culture. The Pre-Socratics had earlier raised this question. Thales, who may have been a Semite (Herodotus, *History* 1.170), opined that the world originates in and returns to water. Heraclitus claimed that the world and life is defined by flux and change, but that inexplicably all was held together by Logos, which he

perceived as transcendent wisdom (Heraclitus did not believe that the cosmos was created; it was an everlasting fire).
The Jewish sages, in ways similar to Thales and Heraclitus,
also sought to comprehend the origin and essence of things.
During the Second Temple period, many Jews found an answer. They concluded that Wisdom was "the fashioner of all
things."

As Socrates and Plato speculated on the source of knowledge in fifth-century Greece, so early Jewish scholars pondered how it was possible to learn and obtain insight. Many
confessed that "what is secret and what is manifest" had been
disclosed by Wisdom, who taught them. Thus, knowledge is
revealed to some humans by Wisdom.

More and more Jewish intellectuals turned to reflect on
Wisdom. Many erudite Jews saw her as a being closest to
God, perhaps someone more significant than an archangel.
Sometime after Octavian defeated Anthony at Actium in 31
B.C.E., a Jew in Alexandria wrote the Wisdom of Solomon.
As the title suggests, he focused on the nature of Wisdom.
He affirmed that she is "a pure emanation of the glory of
the Almighty." She is both "a reflection of eternal light" and
"a spotless mirror of the working of God." She is nothing
less that "an image of his goodness." She passes into human
souls "and makes them friends of God" (Wisdom of Solomon
7:25–27, NRSV).

Reflections on wisdom traditions in Judaism and earliest Christianity shape the five papers collected and edited in
this volume. They were presented during two separate symposia at Florida Southern College. As part of the Faith and
Scholarship Colloquies, they seek to share with all that are
interested some of the discoveries and insights obtained by
learned and established scholars. The papers in this volume
are seminal and thought provoking.

Roland Murphy explores the biblical and Jewish Wisdom literature and focuses on the ways Jews sought to
understand sin and suffering. He examines the deed-and-its-
consequences paradigm found in Proverbs; that is, wisdom

leads to success but folly to disaster. He then places this perspective in conversation with other subsequent Jewish perspectives: (1) Suffering is part of "the mystery of the Lord's doing" (Job); (2) any understanding of sin and suffering is unattainable for humans (Qoheleth); (3) wisdom is tantamount to Torah (Sirach); and (4) the pursuit of wisdom ends in immortality (Wisdom of Solomon).

Peter Schäfer argues that the association of wisdom, Torah, and Israel found in biblical literature was rehearsed much later in the thought of rabbinic sages. After their return from exile, Jews came to believe that prophecy had ceased and began to conceive of Torah as a depository of written revelation rather than a process of instruction. Alongside these developments grew the idea that the universal wisdom praised in Proverbs 8 was uniquely associated with Israel and was, in fact, one and the same with Israel's written Torah (as explained in Sirach). The later rabbis developed three insights: (1) They put themselves and their own oral tradition "on top of" the written Torah; (2) they associated the idea of Torah with that of wisdom; and (3) they interpreted this wisdom, reflected in Torah, to have been given uniquely to Israel.

C. H. Dodd was an influential New Testament scholar at the University of Cambridge during the middle of the twentieth century. He claimed that Philo's writings provided an essential background for the Gospel of John. For Dodd, Jewish wisdom speculation led to Philo's Logos, which, along with other biblical elements, explains John's development and comprehension of the Word (Logos). **Peder Borgen** takes seriously Dodd's suggestion and provides necessary nuances by shifting Dodd's focus from ideas and outlook to Philo's and John's uses of scripture and the social setting of the Gospel of John. Borgen explores how several Johannine themes are understandable when read in light of Philo. He gives special attention to Philo's and John's exegeses of Genesis and Exodus, as well as their respective views on the Sabbath, birth from above, the Temple, and the ascent-descent theme. He then arrives at an array of conclusions that expose the similarities and dissimilarities existing between Philo and John. He clarifies how Philo's interpretation of scripture helps illuminate certain perplexing passages in the Gospel of John.

D. Moody Smith focuses on the historical traditions in the Gospel of John, which is now perceived to be a Jewish composition. He stresses that John's language about the heavenly Christ — or Wisdom — should not imply the lack of historical value in the narrative. Smith summarizes John's probable relation to the Synoptics (Matthew, Mark, and Luke) and reveals the historical value of John by considering several aspects of the Passion Narrative. Smith's primary discussion is a detailed comparison (in conversation with R. E. Brown) of the similarities and differences between John's and Mark's Passion Narratives, interlaced with comments as to their relationship and especially for John's historical value. Smith shows that at many points within the Passion Narrative John differs from the Synoptics. When these differences do not serve John's theological agenda, Smith wisely suggests that we should be open to the possibility that John represents old traditions and perhaps historical facts.

James H. Charlesworth explains how some Jews emphasized that Wisdom did not find a home on earth and other Jews contended that Wisdom found a home within Israel in Torah. The former concept is found in the Jewish apocalypses, the latter in the Jewish Wisdom literature. He argues that both apocalyptic thought and wisdom traditions definitively influenced the author of the Gospel of John. The author of John may have been thinking about Sirach 24:17, which likens wisdom to a vine, when he portrays Jesus as the vine in John 15.

Some common interpretations shape these independent studies. Schäfer, Borgen, and Charlesworth draw attention to the importance of Jewish traditions and hermeneutics for understanding the opening words in John ("in the beginning"). Both Borgen and Charlesworth look at the preexistent and incarnate Word in the prologue of John as a deliberate shift from the feminine Wisdom to the masculine Logos (contrast the view of B. Witherington III, whose position is discussed in chap. 5). Each also sees the importance of a polemic in John 3:13 against those who, like Philo, have visions of ascending or who, like Enoch, are celebrated as the Son of Man who ascended into heaven and knows all secrets. Both Borgen and Smith, in very different ways, develop some of Dodd's insights into the Gospel of John. All contributors show how earlier traditions about wisdom flow into later Jewish (and Christian) traditions. These diachronic studies reveal the continuity of insightful and formative traditions. Many other common insights connect these fresh explorations of the ways traditions are in dialogue and sparkle as if in a spotless mirror. In various ways the Jewish sages left insights that provide nourishment for existence (*viaticum*) for each traveler on life's way (*viator*). Our lives obtain fuller meaning by looking at the traditions reflecting, sometimes opaquely, sometimes pellucidly, before us.

Professor M. A. Daise of William and Mary College helped me edit these contributions and compiled the bibliography. M. Paulus assisted with this work. President Tom Reuschling of Florida Southern College supports the FSC symposia sponsored each year by the FSC religion and philosophy department. I am grateful to the contributors to this collection of papers for their cooperation and superb work, and all those who enable the symposia to continue. Foremost among the latter is Frances DeMott who has helped endow the yearly gatherings that bring together internationally acclaimed experts and attendees into buildings designed by Frank Lloyd Wright.

Chapter 1

Israel's Wisdom: Dialogue between the Sages

Roland Murphy

The Bible is full of tensions: tensions in the very presentation of God as forgiving and also punishing, as present and also absent, as promising and also reneging; one could go on and on. What is our reaction to this? We can not deny the tensions; can we live with them? I would like to explore a tension that is prominent within the wisdom books of the Old Testament and that is not absent from the rest of the Bible. It is the problem of sin and suffering, wrongdoing and punishment. The biblical view is that sin and suffering belong together, and this mentality has not disappeared from modern thought. Many people regard suffering as a punishment for past wrongdoing! This is so, despite other books of the Bible reinterpreting suffering not as a punishment but as a mystery (e.g., the Book of Job) and even as somehow redemptive (Isaiah 53). These different accents must all be heard and appreciated. They derive ultimately from the mystery of God; they are also to be viewed in the light of the dialogue between various biblical authors or books. I do not mean that one book

or author always consciously and deliberately dialogues with
another. The picture is more complicated. In fact, many authors are involved, and the dialogue is carried on in many
parts of many books. It is, on the whole, a wild conversation
that often veers with sudden turns into unsuspected areas,
that often strays from the path that a logical reader prefers to
continue on. But it is dialogue, all the same.

What books are we talking about? In the Hebrew Bible
are three books, generally classified among the Ketuvim or
Writings: Proverbs, Job, and Ecclesiastes (or Qoheleth in Hebrew). Outside of these three are two works grouped among
the apocryphal or deuterocanonical books: Ben Sira (or Ecclesiasticus) and the Wisdom of Solomon. These last two books
were written at the end of the Old Testament period, roughly
within 200 B.C.E. and 50 C.E. One may speak of wisdom influence on other parts of the Hebrew Bible, but these five works
are generally received as wisdom books.

Is it possible to narrow this dialogue so that we are not
roaming over too large a territory? There are several possibilities. We will choose the Book of Proverbs and put it
in dialogue with the other wisdom books.[1] Proverbs is basic since it contains the oldest wisdom in Israel, to be found
mainly in chapters 10–31. It is widely agreed that chapters
1–9 were written as a kind of introduction to the later chapters, probably in the postexilic period after the return from
the Babylonian exile in 539 B.C.E. and the following years.
The earlier portion consists of long wisdom poems urging
the reader to pursue wisdom, which can be identified with
"the fear of the LORD" (1:7), and avoid evil. This broad aim
is conveyed in a most urgent tone and is climaxed by the opposition between Lady Wisdom and Dame Folly. In contrast
to the long poems are the almost staccato-style sayings found
in most of the succeeding chapters (Proverbs 10–31).

The title of the book is *mishle shelomoh,* or "Proverbs of
Solomon," and this calls for some comment. First of all, we lack
any sure evidence for attributing to that famous king these
poems and sayings. The theology of the first nine chapters

reflects a much later stage of Israelite thought. Moreover, the sayings characteristic of chapters 10–31 are not the kind of literature that is easily authored by one man. They suggest many authors because they are insights into various areas of reality (farming, reliability in work, honesty in character, war, and peace), originating over a wide range of experiences. Sayings must attain popularity among a people before they are given the status of proverb — a pithy remark that enshrines a clever observation or recommendation. We have many such proverbs in our own American culture that resonate with the Bible and may ultimately derive therefrom, such as "pride goes before a fall" (cf. Proverbs 11:2; 16:18). They are often quite witty and are couched in language that captures attention: wordplays, alliteration, and so forth. The most striking characteristic of the biblical proverb is the well-known parallelism of expression, whereby the second line continues the thought of the first line, positively or negatively. This has been expressed as "if *a* then *b*"; or "if *a* then all the more *b*." The point is that the second line (and in some cases a third line) does not merely repeat the first line. It intensifies or specifies it, prolonging it in a clever way. Thus, "Many are the plans in the heart, / but it is the decision of the LORD that endures" (19:21). Or, "One person is lavish, yet grows richer; / another withholds what is due, but unto poverty" (11:24). The sages sought to give neat turns in literary style to their observations and to have the right word at the right time: "A word in season, how good it is!" (15:23, NRSV); "like golden apples in silver settings are words spoken at the proper time" (25:11).[2]

The dominant theme of the book is that wisdom brings success, in contrast to folly, which is self-destructive. We can call this a "teaching" that emerges from the totality of the sayings. The teaching is practical, not theoretical; it has to do with conduct and human character, more precisely with moral formation: trustworthiness, honesty, straightforward speech, self-control. In many cases, the lesson flows naturally from the saying, thus, "as the door turns on its hinges, / so the sluggard on the bed" (Proverbs 26:14). At other times

exhortation is explicit: "Entrust your works to the LORD, /
and your plans will succeed" (16:3). In many ways Proverbs is
close in spirit to the Mosaic speeches in Deuteronomy; there
is often the same urgent tone, especially in the opening chapters. One is to attain *life*, just as the choice was offered to
Israel in the words of Deuteronomy 30:19: "I put before you
life and death.... Choose life!³

What was life for the Israelite? It was a happy life in the
here and now, blessed with success and prosperity, a large
family, and dignity in the community. Its opposite was death
or Sheol. The latter term is most often parallel to death. Both
terms represent the netherworld, one's ultimate destination
when life ended. This was not a place of either reward or
punishment — just a "next" world where one eked out a dark
and dreary existence; as Job put it, "the black, disordered
land where darkness is the only light" (10:22). The psalmists
continually describe Sheol as a condition in which one no
longer has a *loving* contact with the Lord ("in Sheol, who
can praise you?"). But Sheol/death was more than a place
localized in the belly of the earth. It was also conceived as
a power, a dynamic force that manifested itself in the adver-
sities of this life. The famous "depths" of Psalm 130 ("out
of the depths I cry to you") are the depths of Sheol, which
has cast its shadow over the psalmist in the form of present
suffering. To the extent that one experiences nonlife in this
world, one is in the grasp of death/Sheol. Hence deliverance
could be expressed in terms of resuscitation, a coming to life:
"O LORD, you brought me up from Sheol!" (30:3). This dynamic metaphor finds a pleasant application in the Song of
Songs 8:6, where the woman proclaims that "love is as strong
as death, / longing as fierce as Sheol" — a vivid portrayal
of the force with which love pursues the beloved. The life/
death horizon of biblical wisdom already presents us with a
tension between opposites, and the resolution of the conflict
between life and death or between justice and wickedness
will be played out in the wisdom books that follow Proverbs,
especially Job and Qoheleth.

The method of the sages is perhaps even more important than the content of their teaching. What is enshrined in the instructions and sayings that were handed down might seem somewhat static, but it is the precipitate of observation, of careful weighing of circumstances that affect one's life. The sage was ever in search of new experiences or insights that might modify past experiences. True, this search was undergirded by an optimistic view of the world as the creation of God. But there was a constant awareness of the differences between human beings, good and bad. If readers are tempted to regard the sayings as mere simplifications, they are mistaken. The sayings are based on astute observation, and this must not be lost from sight. Very often the method outweighs the content, leaving the teaching open to further refinement and challenge by later sages. After all, life was at stake.

The wisdom of Israel has often been compared in a condescending and derivative way with the wisdom of ancient Egypt. Toward the beginning of the twentieth century, remarkable discoveries of Egyptian Wisdom literature were made, perhaps the most famous and certainly the most pertinent being the "Teaching of Amenemope," dated to about the twelfth century B.C.E.[4] There is practically unanimous agreement that this work was known to the author of the recommendations in Proverbs 22:17–23:11. There is the same mixture of instruction and saying that we find in biblical wisdom and a striking similarity in the ideas expressed.

This was certainly a welcome find. But it turned out to be a magnet that attracted too much attention to Egypt and less to what is characteristic of Israelite wisdom. A grid, as it were, was placed over biblical wisdom, and it came to be interpreted in the light of the Egyptian ideal of "justice" (one meaning of the many-sided Egyptian concept *maat*). The dominant thrust was now to discover the "order" that the Egyptians saw inherent in the world.

It is no wonder that study of biblical wisdom went into eclipse, as it were. It was simply not exciting; did not all the proverbs repeat the same old things over and over? Oh yes, there was Job tilting with God, and Qoheleth claiming that all was "vanity." But certainly little dialogue was visible between them. I will not dwell on this detour, as I consider it, because today a more balanced judgment is settling in. Wisdom is not a search for preestablished order. Rather, it focuses on ways to cope with life — a calling upon the lessons of human experience, a reading of human nature and all aspects of creation for deeper practical knowledge. This is a precarious venture, in theory and in praxis; hence, the tensions that arise.

Finally, wisdom is also religious (as was the teaching of Amenemope) and engaged in the effort to understand the mysterious Lord before whom "there is no wisdom, no understanding, no counsel" (Proverbs 21:30). It is against this background that the biblical dialogue can be understood. One can rightly charge the traditional sages of Israel with being overoptimistic, but they were not sloppy thinkers, nor were they simpletons. They recognized their limitations, but they were not reluctant to stake out claims for the good life, success, and prosperity. However, reality itself provided difficult problems, and this is where Job and Qoheleth, still true to the method and goals of wisdom, pushed the traditionalists to the wall. I prefer to say that they purified the entire wisdom movement by the hard questions they asked.

Like every one else, the sages embraced the mind-set that connected sin with suffering. The Psalms provide many examples of this. In the laments the psalmists plead for respite from sufferings that admittedly are due to sinfulness (e.g., Psalms 39:10–11; 40:12; 41:3–4; 51:8). It is the Lord who is responsible for this, even if it is sickness or humans who afflict the psalmist. Hence the cry to God, "Do not reprove me in your anger" (6:1); "why, O LORD, do you stand aloof?" (10:1). But agony appears when the just person suffers despite loyalty to God. If it is so that "my steps have been steadfast in your paths" (17:5), how can the Lord fail to intervene? Hence one can cry out, "Do me justice, O LORD! / For I have walked in integrity" (26:1). This is the kind of lament we shall hear more of in the Book of Job. But the complaint is not more frequent than expressions of trust in the Lord that deliverance will come (Psalms 17:8, 15; 27:9–10).

This association of sin with suffering remained mysterious to all Israelites, as well as to the sage. Some scholars suggest that it can be accounted for by a certain mentality that deeds are inevitably associated with consequences: the bad with bad results; the good with good results. This "deed-consequence" view supposedly lies behind the Israelite understanding of retribution.[5] It can be illustrated by such sayings as Proverbs 26:27, where it is expressed that the one who digs a pit for another to fall into, falls into it instead; the stone comes back on the one who rolls it against another (see also Psalms 7:14–16). Our actions, good and bad, have a boomerang effect. There is something attractive about the idea that sin is destructive and that virtue induces good. Many examples illustrate this process, and I would not deny that it could have played a role in Israelite thought. At the same time, I wonder how long it took anyone to realize that life was simply not that smooth. There was plenty of evidence that the one who dug the hole never fell into it! There was no inflexible order set up for deed and appropriate consequence. Israel could never give up the idea that the Lord was at work in everything that happened, weal or woe (e.g., Amos 3:6; Isaiah 45:7). The notion of deed/consequence has been used as a kind of whipping boy in wisdom research. It suggests the rigidity of logic displayed by the friends of Job, and it boxes God into a system, even if, as is claimed, it is of God's own devising. Hence this (ultimately demeaning) view of reality and divine freedom had to go, exorcised by scholarship and the later Wisdom literature (Job, Qoheleth) that supposedly eliminated it. But was it ever really operative?

We have already begun to see the dialogue that has begun. The calm assessment of the sages concerning success and disaster, virtue and evildoing, was bound to be controverted. The most successful sage, the one who saw deeper than most, was the author of the Book of Job. This genius apparently took over the story of the saintly Job (reflected in Ezekiel 14:14, 20) and made him the protagonist of another, deeply felt, view about suffering. For this he had to choose a person who "feared God and avoided evil" (as is repeated several times in Job 1–2, both by the author and by God). And even better, he is a non-Israelite, a man from the land of Uz (probably somewhere in the southern desert), since wisdom was an international possession. With an uncanny flair for the dramatic, the author visualizes the Lord mustering out the heavenly court, "the sons of God" (1:6), and among the divine retinue of messengers or angels is one named "the satan" (or adversary or chief prosecutor — this is not the New Testament devil). In reply to the Lord's question, the satan has indeed noticed Job in his roaming about the world as a kind of official observer. But he will not accept the Lord's verdict about Job's loyalty. He seems to know only too well the ways of humans, and he claims against the Lord's boast that in reality Job's piety is skin deep. Were he to lose all his possessions, he would blaspheme his Maker. The Lord takes up this challenge of the satan and allows him to inflict damage to all but Job's person. Although Job passes this test, that is not enough for the satan. If Job suffers in his person, he will curse God. The wager is agreed to, and the way is open for the great *literary* battle that is to ensue. For the debate between Job and the three friends is not a historical event that a bystander recorded. It is a literary masterpiece written by a sage who knew both wisdom theory and hard reality.

Job breaks into mighty laments: Why? Why? The attentive reader will find echoes of the Psalms in these complaints. The three friends, all non-Israelites, who came to console him are genuinely overcome at the sight of his suffering; they can only observe an empathetic silence for seven days. But Job's initial lament (3:3–26) is too much for them; they owe it to him and to themselves to bring to bear whatever wisdom can contribute to the alleviation of his suffering. And so Eliphaz begins in a kindly way a lecture that should enable Job to recognize his sinfulness, confess it, and thus be restored by a merciful God. This was sound wisdom (and liturgical, as well), a doctrine that all could accept. Eliphaz, and his friends too, argue backward from suffering to its cause, namely sin. This mentality perdured into the Christian era (as the disciples of Jesus asked when they saw the man born blind: "Was it his sin or that of his parents?"; John 9:2), and indeed it is not absent in our own day. But the author of the Book of Job has deliberately chosen a holy man as the one who suffers; he has no sins to confess. This suffering has come upon him without any cause (Job 2:3). The old remedies cannot apply. And so the debate goes on, back and forth between each of the three friends in turn and Job. The most interesting characteristic is that the friends never lose their style of wisdom teaching: if only Job would learn from the example of the punishment of the wicked! If only he would recognize his own sinfulness! Instead, Job must deny that he is a sinner who has brought these calamities upon himself. He must deny it, if he is a man of integrity. And you, the reader, know this — although neither the friends nor Job are aware of what transpired in chapters 1–2. But Job not only protests that he is innocent; he also attacks God in violent language (cf. 9:22–24). At the same time, in contrast to the professorial style of the three friends who give lectures, he prays to this God. Several of his speeches end with moving appeals:

> Remember that my life is like the wind;
> I shall not see happiness again.
> The eye that now sees me shall no more behold me;
> as you look at me, I shall be gone.
> — Job 7:7–8

As the debate draws to an end, the traditional arguments of the sages yield before the stubborn faith of Job. Even Elihu (Job 32–37) can add little to what has been already said for "orthodoxy." The author now has the boldness to let the Lord speak — but perhaps he felt that he had no other choice after allowing Job in chapter 31 to issue challenges to God for an immediate confrontation (cf. 13:3; 23:3; 31:35). The Lord who takes over in chapter 38 seems quite different from the one that entered the wager with the satan (who never reappears!) in chapters 1–2. In a lofty tone the Lord speaks of the mysteries of creation without really engaging Job except for a brief challenge in 40:8–14: if Job can do better in handling matters, let him take over! Then the Lord launches into the famous description of the symbols of chaos, Leviathan and Behemoth. The lines allotted to Job as a "reply" are few and even ambiguous (40:3–5; 42:1–6). The clearest statement is in 42:5, where Job places great emphasis on his *seeing* God after so much mere hearsay. It seems as though the Lord has no interest in Job's reaction; Job has already proved himself right in what he has said, as opposed to the friends who did not speak "rightly" and for whom Job is told to intercede. In the epilogue (42:7–17) the author does seem to recognize that God can reward faithful followers, for he doubles Job's former possessions (the award for damages according to Exodus 22:4).

Wisdom theology was never quite the same after this. The same thirst for assessing reality remained, but now the mystery of the Lord's doing was ever more to the fore. A definite cloud — not the guiding marker of the exodus march — hung over the issues of personal security and prosperity. The traditional proclamation of the Lord's mercy and concern (Exodus 34:6: "The LORD, a God merciful and compassionate, slow to anger and rich in kindness and fidelity") did not cease to be repeated in the liturgy (Psalms 86:5, 15; 103:8; 145:8), but the hard realities of life could not be ignored either. A sense of crisis was reinforced by the incredible destruction of Jerusalem in 587 B.C.E. and the ensuing exile of the people of God. It is remarkable that this devastating episode did not stir up the doubts and questions one might expect. Instead, it was generally interpreted as punishment for Israel's infidelity. The opening words of Isaiah 40 clearly indicate Israel's sinful responsibility for the cataclysm, although they also proclaim that its exile is about to end. The Deuteronomic interpretation of Israel's history, which colors the books from

Joshua to Kings, crowded out remonstrations such as those voiced by the prophet Habakkuk, who questioned the ways of the Lord on the international level. National calamities did not match the difficulties that Israelites experienced on a personal and individual level. Here the justice of God was more keenly perceived to be a problem, as the Book of Job demonstrates. Yet the wisdom movement remained stubbornly on course: the traditional sayings were gathered together and preserved in the Book of Proverbs. These did not answer all the questions, but who could?

There was one who made a desperate attempt to attain wisdom, and, by his own admission, he failed (Ecclesiastes 7:23–24): Qoheleth, whose message and date have posed many problems to scholars. His message is generally associated with "vanity" or *hebel* (vapor, breath, emptiness, futility, absurdity), the favorite verdict that he applied to so many ventures in life. Some of his remarks are directly applicable to the questions aired in the Book of Job. But he did not delay over the problem of retribution. He recognized outright that "the sinner does evil a hundred times and survives" (8:12; cf. 8:14). Unlike the character Job, he displays little passion. Indeed, he is rather cold in his assessment of this world. But he sees clearly. The main problem is that human beings cannot understand the work of God, which he affirms four times (3:11; 7:13; 8:17; 11:5). God is the puzzle. Indeed, one cannot know from experience — and this is the proper arena of wisdom's investigation — whether one is loved by God or hated (9:1–2), for the just and the evil are treated alike. The human condition is exacerbated by the mortality of human beings. There is the same lot for all: for humans and animals, for wise and foolish, for just and unjust. This lot is portrayed in his famous definition of Sheol: "All that your hand finds to do, do with might, because there is no action, or answer, or knowledge, or wisdom in Sheol where you are going" (9:10). The only positive recommendation he can make is to enjoy whatever comes to you in life (2:24; 3:12–13, 22; 5:18–19; 8:15; 9:7–9). But let there be no mistake about this: it is a *gift* of a God who is quite arbitrary, for God can never be called to account. In words reminiscent of the Book of Job, he reminds us that human beings "cannot contend with one who is stronger" (6:10). Yet Qoheleth never offers folly as an option. He condemns folly at several points (5:3; 6:11; 10:12–15), even though he cannot bring himself to say that wisdom achieves anything of lasting importance. The appraisal of Qoheleth in the added epilogue is more gentle on Qoheleth than he is on himself. There someone praises him for his teaching, and rightly so, but one is left questioning the ease with which the last verse pronounces, "God will bring every deed to judgment, / over all that is hidden, / whether good or evil." Would Qoheleth have put it that way? I do not think so.[6]

The dates of the three books we have discussed cannot be easily determined. As we have seen, only Proverbs 10–31 is generally considered to be preexilic. The majority of scholarly opinion dates the composition of Job after the exile, but this claim can hardly be proved. Qoheleth has been widely considered as influenced by Hellenistic thought and hence to be dated about 300 B.C.E. Yet strong reasons have also been given to put it in the Persian period (roughly 500–300 B.C.E.). At the least, we can maintain that most Wisdom literature received written form in the postexilic era. This is certain for the two books counted among the deuterocanonical or apocryphal works to which we now turn — Ben Sira and the Wisdom of Solomon. These two writings, because of their disputed canonical status, have suffered more "benign neglect" than the three wisdom books of the Hebrew Bible ever experienced. Each has a specific problem that has discouraged its use. For Ben Sira, there is the matter of the text itself; for the Wisdom of Solomon, it is the Greek aura that surrounds it.

We do not possess complete copies of the fifty-one chapters of Ben Sira in its original Hebrew language. Only about two-thirds of the "original" Hebrew have been recovered — a fascinating story that we cannot retell here. But from about the fifth to the beginning of the twentieth century the book was known to the Western world mainly in its Greek dress:

the translation made by Ben Sira's grandson in the second century B.C.E. Hebrew texts were known to Jewish communities during this time and even quoted in Jewish writings, but the Western world knew the book only in Greek and Latin (and a few other) translations. We have now recovered a considerable portion (about two-thirds) of the Hebrew, but this does not make it any easier to establish what Ben Sira originally wrote. A critical text has to be formed on the basis of the Hebrew and the Greek, and the problems are huge. Nonetheless one must recognize the increasing validity of modern vernacular translations such as those of the New Revised Standard Version and the Anchor Bible commentary by P. Skehan and A. Di Lella.[7] Tremendous progress has been made, and it invites a greater readership.

Who was Ben Sira? A devout Jewish scribe who lived most probably in Jerusalem and wrote his book around 180 B.C.E., before the troubles caused by the Greek ruler Antiochus IV Epiphanes and the victorious revolt led by the Maccabee family against Greek domination. Does he show something of this background in his writing? Outside of an impassioned prayer in Sirach 36:1–22, he seems almost to ignore the storm that was doubtless building up in his day. There can be no denying the apprehension shown in the opening lines, "Come to our aid, God of the universe.... / Lift up your hand against foreign peoples" (36:1–3). But by and large his strategy was not militant; it was subtle: to safeguard and to urge loyalty to Jewish traditions by presenting them in the dress of wisdom teaching that promoted "fear of the Lord" and devotion to the Torah.

There is no easy way of summarizing or outlining the teaching of Ben Sira. His work, distributed over fifty-one chapters, does not follow a recognized plan. His grandson, who translated Ben Sira's work into Greek about 130 B.C.E., remarked in the prologue with which he introduced his translation that his grandfather was steeped in the study of the Law, the Prophets, and the "other books." This is quite true. In many ways the work is a repository of traditional wisdom. This is obvious especially in two respects: the forms and the themes found in the book.[8] He adopts, and adapts, many different literary forms, from the short proverbial saying to the lengthy wisdom poem. He is particularly given to composing poems of twenty-two lines, corresponding to the number of letters in the Hebrew alphabet, or variations with twenty-three lines (Sirach 1:11–30; 51:13–30), and there are some outstanding hymns (39:12–35; 42:15–43:33). Short sayings, so characteristic of Proverbs 10–31, do not stand out in Ben Sira, because they are usually worked into larger units. But there are very many of them, whether they were authored or, more likely, collected by him.

While there is real similarity between Ben Sira and Proverbs, there is also a puzzle. One would expect Ben Sira to be shaken by the books of Job and Ecclesiastes, which he must certainly have known. But he remains very much a traditionalist, retaining the connection between sin and suffering as a punishment (e.g., Sirach 5:4–6; 18:21). He affirms the basic goodness of creation (16:24–17:24) and also holds to divine retribution upon human wrongdoing (16:1–23). Like his predecessors, he thought that this must occur in this life, since there was no settling of accounts in the next (Sheol). His themes are familiar to us from the Book of Proverbs: moderation, forgiveness, humility, family relationships, self-control, and so forth. He remained a firm believer in the wisdom tradition, as indicated by his praise of the work of the scribe (39:1–11), which he naturally rates above the task of skilled workers like farmers or potters. But he does not denigrate their work; it is a misnomer to call 38:24–34 a "satire" on trades.

Sirach 24 is duly famous as another treatment of personified Wisdom.[9] Here Ben Sira is clearly dependent upon the portrayal of Lady Wisdom in Proverbs 8, but he gives his own spin to this figure. As in Proverbs 8:22–31, Wisdom is of divine origin and "before all ages." She is immediately invested with authority "over every people and nation," among whom she wishes to take up residence (Sirach 24:6–7). The

Creator bids her to dwell in Jacob, specifically in the Jerusalem Temple where she ministers to the Lord. In the style of Lady Wisdom in Proverbs 8:32–36 she issues an invitation to all to come and partake of what she has to offer. Ben Sira then identifies her with the Torah or law of Moses (Sirach 24:23). This is the first explicit identification that Lady Wisdom receives in the tradition, although she is also defined as "fear of the Lord" in several other places in Ben Sira (e.g., 1:11–30).[10] Scholars discuss whether the wisdom or legal aspect is uppermost in the equation Wisdom = Law. This may not be fair to Ben Sira; in other words, was he aware of such a question? For him Wisdom and Torah came together in the program of moral formation that is common to both areas. The explicit identification of Wisdom and Law occurs in seven passages (15:1; 17:11; 19:20; 21:11; 24:23; 34:8; 45:5) and an implicit identification in twelve passages (1:26; 2:15–16; 6:36; 15:15; 19:24; 24:22; 24:32–33; 32:2–3; 38:34; 44:4; 51:15, 30).[11] Some of the latter may be doubtful, as implicit references often are, but the total impression is that Ben Sira was attached to the Torah and perceived that it did fit with the wisdom tradition that he inherited. The point that I wish to make about Ben Sira is that he provides here another example of inner-wisdom dialogue. He crosses lines, as it were — the invisible line that seems to separate covenant and Law from Wisdom.

The Wisdom of Solomon comes to us from a Jewish author of the Diaspora, conversant with Greek thought, probably living in Alexandria. We are unable to define the date of composition, but an informed guess would be the end of the first century B.C.E. and the opening of the new millennium. The author had a good command of Greek, but he also knew his Bible well, especially in the Greek or Septuagint translation. While betraying no little Greek influence, it is an intensely Jewish book. The style is the familiar parallelism of Hebrew poetry, but also marked with clever inclusions throughout the book — an indication that the work was probably composed in Greek, rather than being a translation.

The Wisdom of Solomon contains three main themes: the gift of immortality, the pursuit of Lady Wisdom, and the Egyptian plagues of the exodus. In view of the general Old Testament understanding of Sheol and the next life, the emphasis on immortality is a striking feature of this book. The author speaks of Hades (sometimes equivalent to Sheol, in his thinking), but not of heaven. Immortality is viewed not as a place or as something inherent to a human being, but as a relationship. In Wisdom of Solomon 1:15 we read that righteousness is undying: one's righteous relationship to the Lord is something that is destined to be gifted with permanent divine presence. Those who disrupt the relationship, and even consider the righteous as fools, thus reject the gift. The poignant realization of their mistake is expressed in a most telling way, when they cry out concerning the righteous person: "This is the one whom we once held as a laughing stock / ... fools that we were.... / See how he is accounted among the sons of God; / how his lot is with the holy ones!" (5:4–5). Immortality is given to those who are judged worthy of being in God's family, living with the "holy ones" or sons of God. For the author, immortality is something positive, given to the righteous. Little interest is expressed in the ultimate fate of the evil; they have refused the gift, destroyed the relationship.[12]

In Wisdom of Solomon 6:22 we are introduced to the nameless speaker who will reveal "what wisdom is and how she came to be." A lengthy description of Lady Wisdom follows. She is always spoken about in the third person, in contrast to Proverbs and Ben Sira where Wisdom herself utters her speeches. Now it is "Solomon," the putative author of the book, who sings her praises. Presumably, because of his reputation for wisdom in the Hebrew Bible, he is the perfect spokesman. Three chapters (7–9) are given over to a unique description of Wisdom. Solomon emphasizes the need to pray in order to receive Wisdom (7:7), and a stirring prayer for this gift occupies all of chapter 9: "Give me Wisdom, who sits by your throne.... / Send her forth from your holy heavens, /

from your glorious throne.... / Who ever learned your counsel, / unless you gave Wisdom, / and sent your holy spirit from on high?" This prayer reveals to us that she is not in Zion, nor is she the Law, but rather the *paredros*, one who sits beside the Lord in glory. And this association is expressed in striking imagery in 7:24–26. She penetrates all things (for she is a spirit, as indicated in 1:6 and 9:17), an aura of the divine might, an effusion of the glory of God, the image of divine goodness. In those verses the writer reaches for the most delicate terms he can find to indicate the extraordinary intimacy of Wisdom with God.

Yet, with this intense description, many of the old traits remain. Thus she manifests the same kind activity as Wisdom in Proverbs 8:31: she finds her delight among human beings because she is a "kindly spirit" — literally a philanthropic spirit (Wisdom of Solomon 1:6: "loving humankind"). At the same time she is apart from God, who "loves" her (8:3), and she knows everything, especially the four cardinal virtues (certainly Greek influence here) in which she instructs human beings: temperance, justice, prudence, and fortitude (8:7). In a bold leap outside of the usual parameters of wisdom, the author then describes her working in history from Adam (10:1) to Moses and the deliverance of the people from Egypt (10:1–21). These were *saved* (the word is repeated continually) by Wisdom. This chapter serves as a sort of preface to an unusual treatment of the plagues and Israel's deliverance from the hands of Pharaoh. The author draws various particular lessons from the exodus experience of Israel. Thus the Lord, for all the overwhelming divine power, governs with restraint, to teach the people that "the just must be kind"; and, in turn, they can hope for remission of their sins (12:18–19).

In view of the previous trends within Wisdom literature, the description of Wisdom's activity in the salvation history (Wisdom of Solomon 11–19) is quite surprising. The world of experience and observation is now the world of history, and the transition is made without any difficulty. Scholars often remark that the exodus experience is a premier paradigm or model for Israel's self-understanding. What was credited to the Lord in the exodus is now credited to Wisdom herself: "The holy people and blameless race — it was she / who delivered them from the nation that oppressed them.... / She gave the holy ones the recompense of their labors, / Conducted them by a wondrous road.... / She took them across the Red Sea" (Wisdom of Solomon 10:15–18, NAB).

We began by stating that we would pursue the tension created by sin and by suffering, and we examined this across the three wisdom books of the Hebrew Bible. With Ben Sira and the Wisdom of Solomon, there was a noticeable digression in their descriptions of Lady Wisdom. But this figure does not clash with the viewpoint of Proverbs. She is in harmony with the optimism that characterizes both books. Ben Sira remains optimistic, even while struggling with the tradition. The author of the Wisdom of Solomon creates a real breakthrough by his affirmation of the gift of immortality and life with God. Only there can the tension be resolved, in the mystery of God's gift, the supreme gift of Wisdom.

Notes

1. For a survey of the research on Proverbs during the past century, see R. N. Whybray, *The Book of Proverbs: A Survey of Modern Study* (History of Biblical Interpretation 1; Leiden: Brill, 1995).

2. Unless otherwise indicated, biblical translations are my own. On parallelism, see the works of R. Alter, *The Art of Biblical Poetry: Biblical Parallelism and Its History* (New York: Basic, 1985), and J. L. Kugel, *The Idea of Biblical Poetry* (New Haven: Yale University Press, 1981). For wordplays, alliteration, and paronomasia in the Book of Proverbs, see T. P. McCreesh, *Biblical Sound and Sense: Poetic Sound Patterns in Proverbs 10–29* (Journal for the Study of the Old Testament Supplement 128; Sheffield: Sheffield Academic Press, 1991).

3. Cf. R. E. Murphy, "The Kerygma of the Book of Proverbs," *Interpretation* 20 (1966): 3–14.

4. See the translation by M. Lichtheim, *Ancient Egyptian Literature: A Book of Readings*, vol. 2: *The New Kingdom* (Berkeley: University of California Press, 1976), 146–63.

5. The "deed-consequence" view is advocated widely in German biblical scholarship; cf., e.g., H. D. Preuss, *Einführung in die alttestamentliche Weisheitsliteratur* (Stuttgart: Kohlhammer, 1987). K. Koch's original 1955 article on the subject was rendered into English by T. H. Trapp as "Is There a Doctrine of Retribution in the Old Testament?" in *Theodicy in the Old Testament* (ed. L. J. Crenshaw; Issues in Religion and Theology 4; Philadelphia: Fortress, 1983), 57–87.

6. Cf. R. E. Murphy, *Ecclesiastes* (Word Biblical Commentary 23A; Dallas: Word, 1992), 126.

7. Cf. P. W. Skehan and A. A. Di Lella, *The Wisdom of Ben Sira* (Anchor Bible 39; New York: Doubleday, 1987). References to the text of Ben Sira should follow the numbering of the Greek text fixed by J. Ziegler in the Göttingen Septuagint and adopted in this commentary and in the New Revised Standard Version.

8. For a brief statement of themes, see R. E. Murphy, *The Tree of Life* (2d ed.; Grand Rapids: Eerdmans, 1996), 73.

9. A summary of the biblical data relative to Lady Wisdom can be found in R. E. Murphy, "The Personification of Wisdom," in *Wisdom in Ancient Israel: Essays in Honour of J. A. Emerton* (ed. J. Day, R. P. Gordon, and H. G. M. Williamson; Cambridge: Cambridge University Press, 1995), 222–33.

10. Cf. J. Haspecker, *Gottesfurcht bei Jesus Sirach* (Analecta biblica 30; Rome: Pontifical Biblical Institute Press, 1967).

11. The data is drawn from E. J. Schnabel, *Law and Wisdom from Ben Sira to Paul: A Tradition Historical Inquiry into the Relation of Law, Wisdom, and Ethics* (Wissenschaftliche Untersuchungen zum Neuen Testament 2/11 and 2/16; Tübingen: Mohr [Siebeck], 1985), 69–77.

12. I think it is better to avoid the phrase *immortality of the soul* in this connection; for a contrary view, see D. Winston, "Solomon, Wisdom of," in *Anchor Bible Dictionary* (ed. D. N. Freedman et al.; New York: Doubleday, 1992), 6.123. The author does not reason to immortality from the intrinsic nature of the soul as something that continues to live since it is "spirit." This Greek idea may have acted as a catalyst in his thought, but when he comes to express his notion of immortality, he follows a different route, that of righteousness. Hebrew *nefesh*, or life force, lies behind the author's Greek term *psychē*, which we translate, *faute de mieux*, as "soul."

Chapter 2

Wisdom Finds a Home: Torah as Wisdom

Peter Schäfer

In 538 B.C.E. the Persian king Cyrus issued his famous edict, which made possible and inaugurated the return
of the people of Israel from the Babylonian exile to its promised land. Not by accident is he hailed as God's Messiah, his
anointed one, who acted on behalf of God and gave Israel's
destiny a decisive turn:

> Thus said the LORD to Cyrus, His anointed one (*limshikho*) —
> Whose right hand He has grasped,
> Treading down nations before him.
> . . . .
> For the sake of My servant Jacob,
> Israel My chosen one,
> I call you by name,
> I hail you by title, though you have not known Me.
> I am the LORD and there is none else;
> Beside Me, there is no god.
> I engird you, though you have not known Me,
> So that they may know, from east to west,
> That there is none but Me.
> — Isaiah 45:1–6[1]

Whatever Cyrus had in mind when he granted permission to the Jewish exiles to return to the land of Israel and to rebuild the Jerusalem Temple, there can be no doubt that the period of this return generated far-reaching changes in the way Israel perceived itself and its task in the course of history. There are two main areas in which these changes can be seen.

First, the postexilic period is characterized by the increasing awareness that the era of prophecy (i.e., of actual revelation) was irrevocably terminated.[2] When precisely this notion of the end of prophecy originated, cannot be determined; it would also be inappropriate to look for a clearly defined borderline, because we are no doubt dealing here with a prolonged process that still has its roots in the Hebrew Bible. For example, we read in the Book of Psalms:

> They made Your sanctuary go up in flames;
>> they brought low in dishonor the dwelling-place of Your presence.
> They resolved, "Let us destroy them altogether!"
> They burned all God's tabernacles in the land.
> No signs appear for us;
>> there is no longer any prophet;
>> no one among us knows for how long.
>> — Psalms 74:7–9

Here, the destruction of the Temple (i.e., the First Temple) is obviously linked with the end of prophecy. A similar connection can be found in the Book of Lamentations, which moreover combines the end of prophecy with the end of proper instruction (*torah*):

> Her (Jerusalem's) gates have sunk into the ground,
> He has smashed her bars to bits;
> Her king and her leaders are in exile,
> Instruction (*torah*) is no more;
> Her prophets, too, receive
> No vision from the LORD.
>> — Lamentations 2:9

The (noncanonical) First Book of Maccabees, written about 100 B.C.E., takes up this line of argument and has the

Maccabees deciding about the burnt offering altar in the
Temple, which was profaned by the Seleucids:

> They deliberated over what they should do with the profaned
> altar of the burnt offering, and they came up with the good
> idea of dismantling it lest the fact that the gentiles had defiled it
> should be held to their disgrace. Accordingly, they dismantled
> the altar, and put its stones away on the temple mount in a
> suitable place until a prophet should come to give an oracle
> concerning them.
>
> — 1 Maccabees 4:44–46[3]

Accordingly, it is said about Simon the Maccabee when he
was appointed high priest (1 Maccabees 14:41): "The Jews
and their priests confirmed Simon as their leader and high
priest in perpetuity until a true prophet should appear" (REB).

These and similar passages clearly express an awareness
that prophecy as part of God's revelation has come to an end.
The later rabbis, who of course knew all these traditions, suggested different dates for the termination of prophecy: the
destruction of the First Temple (587 B.C.E.);[4] the death of the
last prophets Haggai, Zechariah, and Malachi (second half
of the sixth century B.C.E.);[5] or the beginning of Greek rule
in Palestine under Alexander the Great (died 323 B.C.E.).[6] All
these dates are only different at first sight: their common de-
nominator is the destruction of the Temple, because the rabbis
on the one hand moved the activity of the last prophets forward to the last days of the Temple[7] and, on the other hand,
let the beginning of Greek rule in Palestine coincide with the
death of these last prophets[8] — a clear chronological anachro-
nism guided by the conception that the cessation of prophecy
was connected with the destruction of the First Temple. This
indicates that the rabbis were aware that the notion of a termination of actual revelation originated during the exile and
was reinforced during the Hellenistic period.

Second, during the postexilic period, a far-reaching
change in the concept of Torah took place. The Hebrew
word *torah* originally meant simply "instruction, teaching,
custom";[9] for example: "An intelligent son heeds instruction

(*torah*), / But he who keeps company with gluttons disgraces his father" (Proverbs 28:7). Torah, therefore, is nothing but a single instruction or, when collected in a list, a collection of instructions. This changes when the emphasis is put not so much on the individual instruction (which can be of varied importance), but on the essence of all the instructions, on the whole complex of teachings and traditions, which, moreover, is written down in a (single) book (Hebrew *sefer*). Now one can deal with this Torah, take it in one's hand, be absorbed with it. In other words, Torah becomes the essence of revelation, the authoritative object of study and sermon and part of the service, in the center of which the reading and explanation of *the* (one) Torah stand.

This important change, which marks the transition from biblical to postbiblical Judaism, is graphically described in the books of Ezra and Nehemiah. Ezra, after his return from Babylon, is characterized as follows: "That Ezra came up from Babylon, a scribe expert in the Teaching (*torah*) of Moses which the Lord God of Israel had given" (Ezra 7:6). Hence, the Torah is accessible in a book — a book, moreover, which is given by God, and the *sofer* (scribe) knows this book and explains it. This latter point, that it is the task of the scribe to explain the book of the Torah, becomes even more apparent: "For Ezra had dedicated himself to study the Teaching (*torah*) of the Lord so as to observe it, and to teach laws and rules to Israel" (7:10).

The Book of Nehemiah describes a scene that some scholars interpret as the first account of a public service in which the Torah, as a book, plays a central role (Nehemiah 8:1–9).[10] The people of Israel assemble on a big square and ask Ezra the scribe to get the book (scroll) containing the Torah of Moses (*sefer torat mosheh*). Ezra brings the book of the Torah in front of the assembly and reads aloud publicly "from first light until midday," and "the ears of all the people were given to the scroll of the Teaching (*torah*)" (8:3). This reading is clearly liturgical in character, because Ezra — standing on a pulpit — opens the book in front of all of the people,

who rise when he opens it (8:5). He begins the reading with
a prayer to which the people respond "Amen, Amen" (8:6).
Then follows the instruction by the Levites ("and the Levites
explained the Teaching [*torah*] to the people"; 8:7), and the
episode concludes with the sentence: "They read from the
scroll of the Teaching (*torah*) of God, translating it (*meforash*)[11]
and giving the sense (*wesom sekhel*); so they understood the
reading" (8:8).

Hence, the Torah is contained in one book and is the
essence of all instruction and teaching; in other words, of Judaism itself. Its reading and explanation belong together. Text
and interpretation are the two poles of a spectrum, the individual elements of which do not exist independently but only
in relation to each other.[12] The unchangeable and invariable
text of the Torah and the changeable and variable explanation
are related in such a way that the text by itself, so to speak,
is irrelevant inasmuch as it exists only as the substratum of
the explanation. Accordingly, the explanation alone is irrelevant and exists only in relation to the text. The written text
of the Torah is always the same, yet changes through the explanation or tradition, which adapts it to ever new historical
circumstances.

What I have described here, or rather what the scene
in Nehemiah 8 (especially 8:8) describes, is the essence of
later rabbinic interpretation of scripture as expressed in the
word *midrash*. As a matter of fact, Ezra 7:10 has precisely this
meaning: "For Ezra had dedicated himself to study the Teaching (*torah*) of the LORD." The Hebrew word *lidrosh* (to study)
means also "to explain, interpret," and this word is related
to the noun *midrash* (interpretation, explanation). Midrash, in
its comprehensive sense, means the principle of the ongoing
and continuous explication of scripture, the different (oral or
literary) forms of this explanation of the written text of the
Bible, and, eventually, the written works that contain these
interpretations.[13]

Finally, most crucial for the change in the understanding
of the Torah in the postexilic period is the adaptation of the

concept of wisdom in early Judaism.[14] Torah — as the source of revelation, the essence of teaching and instruction in one book that never changes and yet is continually changed, through interpretation, in time and history — becomes the embodiment of wisdom. In what follows I will outline some important aspects in this dynamic relation between Torah and wisdom in ancient Judaism.

The earliest detailed praise of Wisdom can be found in Proverbs 8. This chapter belongs to the latest stage of the redaction of the Book of Proverbs, probably soon after the Babylonian exile.[15] Here, Wisdom is the essence of all knowledge and success; she was created by God in primeval times as his sole companion before he created the world:

> The LORD created me at the beginning of His course
> As the first of His works of old.
> In the distant past I was fashioned,
> At the beginning, at the origin of earth.
> There was still no deep when I was brought forth,
> No springs rich in water;
> Before [the foundation of] the mountains were sunk,
> Before the hills I was born.
> He had not yet made earth and fields,
> Or the world's first clumps of clay.
> I was there when He set the heavens into place;
> When He fixed the horizon upon the deep;
> When He made the heavens above firm,
> And the fountains of the deep gushed forth;
> When He assigned the sea its limits,
> So that its waters never transgress His command;
> When He fixed the foundations of the earth,
> I was with Him as a confidant (*amon*),
> A source of delight every day,
> Rejoicing before Him at all times,
> Rejoicing in His inhabited world,
> Finding delight with mankind.
> — Proverbs 8:22–31

But how does Wisdom reach the world? How does she come close to humankind (Proverbs 8:31)? She is with God, and yet she reaches the world and talks to people in the

streets and squares of the city: "Wisdom cries aloud in the
streets, / Raises her voice in the squares. / At the head of
the busy streets she calls; / At the entrance of the gates,
in the city, she speaks out" (1:20–21). Everyone who listens
to her "finds life / And obtains favor from the LORD. / But
he who misses me destroys himself; / All who hate me love
death" (8:35–36). Hence, Wisdom is life; refusal of Wisdom
means death.

This concept of Wisdom is adopted at the beginning of
the second century B.C.E. (around 190/180 B.C.E.) by the Wisdom of Ben Sira (Jesus son of Sirach or Ecclesiasticus), which
was translated into Greek around 132 B.C.E. by Ben Sira's
grandson, who lived in Egypt.[16] Here Wisdom praises herself again, and again she is created before the creation of the
world:[17]

> Wisdom sings her own praises,
>   among her own people she proclaims her glory;
> In the assembly of the Most High she opens her mouth,
>   in the presence of his host she declares her worth:
> "From the mouth of the Most High I came forth,
>   and mistlike covered the earth.
> In the heights of heaven I dwelt,
>   my throne on a pillar of cloud.
> The vault of heaven I compassed alone,
>   through the deep abyss I took my course.
> . . . .
> Before the ages, from the first, he created me,
>   and through the ages I shall not cease to be."
>   — Sirach 24:1–5, 9

But it is precisely within this praise of universal wisdom that
the author of Ben Sira adds a new and crucial detail: Wisdom
finds her appropriate place among one particular people:

> Over waves of the sea, over all the land,
>   over every people and nation I held sway.
> Among them all I sought a resting place:
>   in whose inheritance should I abide?
> Then the Fashioner of all gave me his command,
>   and he who had made me chose the spot for my tent,

> Saying, "In Jacob make your dwelling,
>   in Israel your inheritance."
> . . . .
> In the holy Tent I ministered before him,
>   and then in Zion I took up my post.
> In the city he loves as he does me, he gave me rest;
>   in Jerusalem my domain.
> I have struck root among the glorious people;
>   in the portion of the Lord is my inheritance.
>   — Sirach 24:6–8, 10–12

Israel is the privileged place of Wisdom, before all other peoples and nations, because it is the privileged and chosen people of God. And then Ben Sira explains how Wisdom reaches Israel. She does not stand any more in the gates and the streets of cities; she can be found in one single and authoritative book, the same book from which Ezra read in front of the people of Jerusalem:

> All this is the book of the covenant of God Most High (*tauta
>   panta biblos diathēkēs theou hypsistou*),[18]
> "the Law which Moses enjoined on us (*nomon hon eneteilato
>   hēmin Mōysēs*)
> as a heritage for the community of Jacob."
> It is brimful, like the Pishon, with wisdom —
>   like the Tigris at the time of the new crops.
> It runs over, like the Euphrates, with understanding;
>   like the Jordan at harvesttime.
> It floods, like the Nile, with knowledge (*paideian*);
>   like the Gibon at vintage time.
> The first human never knew wisdom fully,
>   nor will the last succeed in fathoming her.
> Deeper than the sea are her thoughts;
>   her counsels, than the great abyss.
>   — Sirach 24:23–29

"All this" that we have learned about Wisdom, "all this" is the "book of the covenant of God": Wisdom *is* the "book of the covenant," which is identical with the "Law (*nomos*) which Moses enjoined on us." Wisdom is a book, the written Torah, that is to be explained and fathomed, yet can never be exhausted. Wisdom finds her home among one people, Israel, and in one book, the Torah. But this one written book is full of meanings, exposing itself in order to be expounded and uncovering its many layers of knowledge. In other words, the written book of Wisdom or, in later rabbinic terminology the Written Torah, requires its counterpart, without which it cannot exist: the explanation or, in rabbinic terminology, the Oral Torah:

> Now I, like a rivulet from her stream,
>   channeling the waters forth into a garden,
> Said to myself, "I will water my plants,
>   my flower bed I will drench";
> And suddenly this rivulet of mine became a river,
>   then this stream of mine, a sea.
> Again will I send my teachings (*paideian*) forth shining like the
>   dawn,
>   to spread their brightness afar off.
> Again will I pour out instruction (*didaskalian*) like prophecy,
>   and bequeath it to generations yet to come.
> — Sirach 24:30–33

The Written and Oral Torah are dependent on each other (as we have already seen in Nehemiah); the Wisdom of the book pours itself into an abundance of teaching and has finally replaced prophecy. The rabbis of classical rabbinic Judaism have not only brought this idea to a grandiose fruition, they also have put themselves on top of it. They are the ones who in the end guarantee that the abundance of teaching is directed into the right channels, so to speak; that it does not flood — and destroy — everything. This principle could not be better expressed than in the famous beginning of the tractate *Avot*, the "Sayings of the Fathers": "Moses received (the) Torah from Sinai and handed it on to Joshua, and Joshua to the elders, and the elders to the prophets, and the prophets handed it on to the men of the Great Assembly" (*Avot* 1.1).[19] From Moses, Joshua, the seventy elders, the prophets, and the men of the Great Assembly the unbroken succession proceeds with Simon the Just, Antigonus from Sokho, and the so-called five pairs (*zugot*), with Hillel and Shammai, Gamaliel I and his son Simon b. Gamaliel I, until it finally culminates in

Rabbi Yehuda ha-Nasi (the Patriarch), who is none other than the editor of the Mishnah (about 200 C.E.) and regarded as the climax of rabbinic Judaism. Hence, the rabbis are the true and legitimate successors of Moses and the prophets; their Oral Torah (i.e., their interpretation of the Torah) *is* the Torah of Moses. A wonderful story in the Babylonian Talmud makes this principle very clear:[20]

> Rab Judah said in the name of Rab, When Moses ascended on high he found the Holy One, blessed be He, engaged in affixing coronets to the letters [of the Torah; i.e., *tagin* or small strokes written on top of certain letters in the form of a crown]. Said Moses, "Lord of the Universe, Who stays Thy hand [i.e., is there anything wanting in the Torah that these additions are necessary]?" He answered, "There will arise a man, at the end of many generations, Akiva b. Joseph by name, who will expound upon each tittle heaps and heaps of laws." "Lord of the Universe," said Moses; "permit me to see him." He replied, "Turn thee round." Moses went and sat down behind eight rows [of Aqiva's disciples, and listened to the discourses upon the law]. Not being able to follow their arguments he was ill at ease, but when they came to a certain subject and the disciples said to the master, "Whence do you know it?" and the latter replied, "It is a law given unto Moses at Sinai," he was comforted. Thereupon he returned to the Holy One, blessed be He, and said, "Lord of the Universe, Thou hast such a man and Thou givest the Torah by me!" He replied, "Be silent, for such is My decree!" (Babylonian Talmud, *Menaḥot* 29b)

The rabbis were also very aware of the early connection between Wisdom and Torah described above. As a matter of fact, I argue that this connection is one of the fundamental principles of rabbinic Judaism. It was codified in the early Aramaic translation of the first sentence of the Book of Genesis and in the midrashic literature. The very beginning of the Hebrew Bible in the Book of Genesis has been a challenge for many generations of readers: *Bereshit bara elohim et hashamayim weet haarets.* One of the crucial questions is, What does this *bereshit* mean? The Septuagint understood it temporally: *En archē epoiēsen ho theos ton ouranon kai tēn gēn* (in the beginning God created the heaven and the earth), and this is also the translation, for instance, of the Revised English Bible. (The Greek translation by Aquila is even more literal in translating *bereshit* with *en kephalaiō*.) Most of the Aramaic Bible translations follow this interpretation. For example, the Targum Onqelos reads *beqadmin bera yy yat shemayya weyat ara* (in the beginning [very long ago] God created the heavens and the earth). And the so-called Targum Pseudo-Jonathan has *min awwla* (in primeval times).

This, however, is not the only possible translation. The so-called Fragmentary Targum translates *bekhokmah bera yy yat shemayya weyat ara* (in [*or* by means of] wisdom God created the heavens and the earth). Interestingly enough, the so-called Codex Neofiti combines both possibilities and translates: *millqadmin bekhokmah* (from the beginning with [*or* by means of] wisdom God created and perfected the heavens and the earth).[21] There can be no doubt that the original meaning of this translation is not "in wisdom (i.e., in his own wisdom) God created the heavens and the earth," but rather "by means of wisdom." This can be demonstrated by a midrash that makes this meaning very clear: "R. Oshaya commenced (his exposition of Genesis 1:1 with the help of the following verse): I was with Him as a confidant, a source of delight every day (Proverbs 8:30)" (*Genesis Rabbah* 1.1 on Genesis 1:1). This verse is a quotation from Proverbs 8:30. The new Jewish Publication Society Version, which I quote, renders Hebrew *amon* as "confidant," but this word is by no means clear (Revised English Bible has "darling"). What the midrash does, therefore, is to define or rather mark out the range of the possible meanings of *amon:*

> *Amon* means tutor,
> *amon* means covered,
> *amon* means castigated;
> and some say: *amon* means great.
> *amon* is a tutor, as Scripture says: "As a nursing father (*haomen*) carrieth the sucking child" (Numbers 11:12);
> *amon* means covered, as Scripture says: "They were clad (i.e., covered: *haemunim*) in scarlet" (Lamentations 4:5);

amon means castigated, as Scripture says: "He was foster father (*omen*) to Hadassah" (Esther 2:7);

amon means great, as Scripture says: "Art thou better than No-amon" (Nahum 3:8)? which is rendered [in the Aramaic Bible translation]: "Art thou better than Alexandria the Great, that is situated among the rivers?"
— *Genesis Rabbah* 1.1 on Genesis 1:1

So far the midrash is, if I may say so, an exercise in ancient philology. As usual, it saves until the end the most important possible interpretation of *amon*, the one that really matters:

Another interpretation: *amon* is a workman (or an architect: *uman*). The Torah declares: "I was the working tool of the Holy One, blessed be He." In human practice, when a mortal king builds a palace, he builds it not with his own skill but with the skill of an architect. The architect moreover does not build it out of his head, but employs plans and diagrams to know how to arrange the chambers and the wicket doors. Thus God consulted the Torah and created the world. And the Torah declares: "*Bereshit* God created" (Genesis 1:1), and *reshit* refers to the Torah, as in the verse: "The Lord made me at the *reshit* of His course" (Proverbs 8:22). (*Genesis Rabbah* 1.1 on Genesis 1:1)

Let me explain this midrash in some detail. It has the form of a homily in which the combination of two different verses of the Bible is essential. It is the art of the author or rather preacher (this kind of homily was probably delivered as a sermon during the synagogue service) to combine two biblical verses that at first sight do not seem to have anything to do with each other (this is definitely the case in our example: there is no obvious connection between Genesis 1:1 and Proverbs 8:30), but that in the end, after his explanation, appear in a new light.[22]

So what new light does Proverbs 8:30 throw on our understanding of Genesis 1:1? The midrash begins by listing the different possibilities for explaining the difficult word *amon* in Proverbs 8:30, none of which are crucial for its interpretation except for the last one: *amon* means workman or architect. The following parable then shows that the Torah was the worker or architect and, at the same time, also the tool of God, that he used when creating the world. The proof of this is 8:22, which is explained in a double way: First it proves that the speaker of 8:22 (Wisdom) was with God from the very beginning, in primeval times, before he created heaven and earth; second, because 8:22 uses the same word (*reshit*) as in Genesis 1:1, we may transfer the subject of Proverbs 8:22 (Wisdom) to Genesis 1:1. *Bereshit* in Genesis 1:1, therefore, can mean only "by means of *reshit* — by means of wisdom" (which is Torah, as we know from Jesus Sirach) God created the world. Here, then, we have the exegetical operation of which the Aramaic Bible translation communicates the result: the Torah is God's tool of creation in the sense that he literally looked into the book of the Torah and used it as the building plan of the world.

Everything that is said about Wisdom in the early texts is true also for the Torah: it is the source of life and includes in it the whole world or rather the entire cosmos. Torah is world, and world is Torah. If God used the Torah as his building plan it is only natural that those, and only those, who read and understand (and fulfill!) the Torah in the proper sense are in harmony with God's creation. Since Wisdom, which is Torah, is given to Israel, it is Israel to whom this task of understanding and fulfilling of the Torah is entrusted: "Beloved are Israel, for to them was given a precious implement. Extraordinary is the love made known to them that they were given the precious implement with which the world was created, as it is said [in scripture]: For I give you good doctrine (*leqakh tob*),[23] do not forsake my teaching (*torati*) (Proverbs 4:2)" (*Avot* 3.23).[24] The people of Israel, with the rabbis at their head, are the vanguard of the nations of the world. They have the precious tool in their hands with which the world was created, and it therefore depends on them which direction the world will take. From here it is only a small step to the notion of later Jewish mysticism that it is Israel's (and only Israel's) duty to restore the world to its original order, before it was disturbed and destroyed by human inclination to sin. Hence, Israel's destiny takes on cosmic dimension: since only they have in their hands the key to the cosmos, it is only they who can lead the cosmos to its destined end.

Such a far-reaching concept of wisdom and Torah could not remain unchallenged, and we have evidence, indeed, that the rabbis were challenged. They answered with a whole set of midrashim explaining why the Torah was given to Israel and not to the nations. The climax of their different answers is the following midrash:[25]

> And it was for the following reason that the nations of the world were asked to accept the Torah: In order that they should have no excuse for saying: Had we been asked we would have accepted it. For, behold, they were asked and they refused to accept it, for it is said: "And he said: 'The Lord came from Sinai,' " etc. ("He shone upon them from Seir; He appeared from Mount Paran") (Deuteronomy 33:2). (*Mekilta* on Exodus 20:2)

The introduction of the midrash sets the tone: the nations of the world cannot argue that they have been deliberately excluded from keeping the Torah because it was not offered to them but only to Israel. On the contrary, Deuteronomy 33:2 proves, according to the interpretation of the midrash, that God appeared not only on Sinai (where he finally gave the Torah to Israel), but also on Seir and Paran. Seir is connected with Esau, Jacob's brother, who in rabbinic literature symbolizes the Gentile nations (whereas Jacob, of course, stands for Israel); for instance, in Genesis 32:4: "Jacob sent messengers ahead to his brother Esau in the land of Seir, the country of Edom." That God appeared also on Seir (and Paran) can mean only, therefore, that he offered the Torah to Esau and to the representatives of other nations before he offered it to Israel. And the midrash explains this in more detail in the following:

> He appeared to the children of Esau the wicked (Esau is often called "the wicked" in rabbinic literature because he is the opponent of Jacob = Israel)[26] and said to them: "Will you accept the Torah?" They said to Him: "What is written in it?" He said to them: "Thou shalt not murder" (Deuteronomy 5:17). They then said to Him: "The very heritage which our father left us

was: 'And by your sword shall you live' " (Genesis 27:40; this is part of Isaac's blessing on Esau).

He then appeared to the children of Amon and Moab. He said to them: "Will you accept the Torah?" They said to Him: "What is written in it?" He said to them: "Thou shalt not commit adultery" (Deuteronomy 5:18). They, however, said to Him that they were all of them children of adulterers, as it is said: "Thus were both the daughters of Lot with child by their father" (Genesis 19:36; Amon and Moab, the children of Lot's daughters, became the progenitors of the nations of the Ammonites and the Moabites; strictly speaking, they were born of incest and not of adultery, since Lot's daughters were not married).

Then He appeared to the children of Ishmael. He said to them: "Will you accept the Torah?" They said to Him: "What is written in it?" He said to them: "Thou shalt not steal" (Deuteronomy 5:19). They then said to Him: "The very blessing that had been pronounced upon our father was: 'And he shall be as a wild ass of a man: his hand shall be upon everything' (Genesis 16:12; this is taken literally; i.e., he will steal everything). And it is written: 'For, indeed, I was stolen away out of the land of the Hebrews' " (40:15; the one who speaks here is Joseph, who, strictly speaking, was not stolen but sold to the Ishmaelites who brought him to Egypt; see 37:28).

But when He came to the Israelites and "at His right hand was a fiery law unto them" (Deuteronomy 33:2; i.e., the Torah, which he offered to them), they all opened their mouths and said: "All that the Lord hath spoken will we do and obey (*naaseh wenishma*)" (Exodus 24:7). And thus it [scripture] says: "He stood and measured the earth; He beheld and drove asunder the nations" (Habakkuk 3:6; i.e., after they refused to accept the Torah). (*Mekilta* on Exodus 20:2)

This is a beautifully structured midrash. God, indeed, offered the Torah first to the representatives of the nations before he offered it to Israel. Every nation refused it because of one peculiar command, the transgression of which is characteristic of this particular nation. The first is Esau, who especially symbolizes the Roman Empire (both the pagan and later the Christian Roman Empire), the major enemy of Israel during the rabbinic period.[27] Rome cannot accept the Torah because it lives by the sword; that is, conquers other nations and oppresses them. Next come Amon and Moab, who are committed to adultery because they are born in adultery. The third nation to be offered the Torah by God is the Ishmaelites. They descended from Ishmael, the son of Abraham with Hagar, his wife Sarah's maidservant, who became the progenitor of the Arabs.[28] They cannot accept the Torah because they are accustomed to stealing. Hence, three major prohibitions among the Ten Commandments — murder, adultery, and robbery (which according to the rabbis apply also to the Gentiles)[29] — cannot be accepted by the heads of the nations.

Then comes the climax: Israel. All the nations, after being asked by God whether they accept the Torah, reply with the counterquestion: "What is written in it?" Only Israel, when God shows them the Torah (he does not even ask, he just shows it to them), says immediately, without asking anything: "All that the Lord has spoken will we do and obey." The words translated "will we do and obey" literally mean "will we do *and hear.*" That is, Israel does not ask God, as the nations did, what the Torah contains; they are ready to fulfill the Torah ("will we do") *before* they have heard what is written in it ("and hear": we accept doing it before we have heard it). This is what distinguishes Israel from the nations and explains why they, and only they, possess the Torah. The nations may now be jealous of Israel since they are honored with the Torah, and they may now understand what they miss, but they deserve it because they have rejected it. The nations have missed, so to speak, their moment in history; they have left the task of saving the world through fulfillment of the Torah to Israel.

The cosmic significance of the Torah, which originates in the equation Torah = Wisdom, runs counter to the notion of the Torah as *nomos* (law), or at least counter to a certain understanding of the Torah as law. As we have seen, the author of Ben Sira matches Wisdom with the book of the covenant, which is "the law (*nomos*) which Moses enjoined on us" (Sirach 24:23); and his grandson, who translated the book into Greek, distinguishes in his prologue for the first time

between the three parts of the Hebrew Bible: "Law" (*nomos*),
Prophets, and the "other Writings of our ancestors." Neither
Sira nor his grandson had any problem calling the Torah *nomos*
because they were only too aware of the close link between
nomos and Wisdom as a cosmic force determining the history
of humankind. It was later, and especially in Christianity, that
the cosmic aspect of Torah was forgotten, or deemphasized,
and that Torah was reduced to a narrowly defined pool of
laws, so to speak, which humans labor in vain to obey. Torah
as Wisdom, as the tool with which God created the world and
which humans use in order to bring the world to its comple-
tion, helps us in understanding the fullness and richness of
a concept that has ramifications not only for Judaism.

Notes

1. Unless otherwise noted, all translations from the Hebrew
Bible are from *Tanakh: A New Translation of the Holy Scriptures according
to the Traditional Hebrew Text* (Philadelphia: Jewish Publication Society,
1985).
2. For more detail, see E. E. Urbach, "Matai pasqah ha-nevu'ah?"
Tarbiz 17 (1945/46): 1–11; and P. Schäfer, *Die Vorstellung vom Heiligen
Geist in der rabbinischen Literatur* (Munich: Kösel, 1972), 143–46.
3. Translation from J. A. Goldstein, *I Maccabees* (Anchor Bible
41; Garden City: Doubleday, 1976), 272.
4. Babylonian Talmud, tractate *Yoma* 21b; Jerusalem Talmud,
tractates *Ta'anit* 2.1 folio 65a and *Horayot* 3.3 folio 47c; *Song of Songs
Rabbah* 8.9, 3; *Exodus Rabbah* 15.10.
5. Tosefta, tractate *Sotah* 13.2–3; Jerusalem Talmud, tractate
Sotah 9.13/14, folio 24b.
6. *Seder 'Olam Rabbah* 30 in *Seder 'Olam Rabba* (ed. B. Ratner;
Vilnius: Romm, 1897), 139–40; and *Seder 'Olam Zuta* in *Seder 'Olam
Zuta* (ed. M. Gnossberg; London: n.p., 1910), 26–27.
7. *Pesiqta of Rab Kahana* in *Pesikta de Rav Kahana* (ed. M. Mandel-
baum; New York: Jewish Theological Seminary of America, 1962), 238.
8. *Seder 'Olam Zuta*, 26–27.
9. Cf. W. Gutbrod, in "Νόμος," *Theological Dictionary of the New
Testament* (ed. G. Kittel; trans. G. W. Bromiley; Grand Rapids: Eerd-

mans, 1967), 4.1044–47; and W. Harvey, "Torah," in *Encyclopaedia Judaica* (Jerusalem: Encyclopaedia Judaica, 1971), 15.1235.

10. C. Perrot sees in Nehemiah 8:1–2 "the prefiguration of the synagogue"; see "The Reading of the Bible in the Ancient Synagogue," in *Mikra: Text, Translation, Reading, and Interpretation of the Hebrew Bible in Ancient Judaism and Early Christianity* (ed. M. J. Mulder and H. Sysling; Compendia rerum iudaicarum ad Novum Testamentum 2.1; Assen: Van Gorcum/Philadelphia: Fortress, 1988), 137–59, quotation from 149.

11. "Translating it" (*meforash*) in the New Jewish Publication Society Version could be better rendered as "explaining it." The rabbinic interpretation (cf. Jerusalem Talmud, tractate *Megillah* 4.1 folio 74d; Babylonian Talmud, tractates *Megillah* 3a and *Nedarim* 37b; *Genesis Rabbah* 36.8) understands the explanation of the Torah as the Aramaic translation (Targum).

12. On this fundamental principle of the close and inseparable relationship between text and interpretation in Judaism, see M. Fishbane, *Biblical Interpretation in Ancient Israel* (Oxford: Clarendon, 1985), 6–13; and P. Schäfer, "Text, Auslegung und Kommentar im rabbinischen Judentum," in *Text und Kommentar* (ed. J. Assmann and B. Gladigow; Archäologie der literarischen Kommunikation 4; Munich: Fink, 1995), 166.

13. Cf. H. L. Strack and G. Stemberger, *Introduction to the Talmud and Midrash* (trans. M. Bockmuehl; Edinburgh: T. & T. Clark, 1991), 255–58.

14. Cf. E. J. Schnabel, *Law and Wisdom from Ben Sira to Paul: A Tradition Historical Inquiry into the Relation of Law, Wisdom, and Ethics* (Wissenschaftliche Untersuchungen zum Neuen Testament 2/11 and 2/16; Tübingen: Mohr [Siebeck], 1985); and M. Hengel, *Judentum und Hellenismus* (3d ed.; Wissenschaftliche Untersuchungen zum Neuen Testament 10; Tübingen: Mohr [Siebeck], 1988), 284–90; cf. also the following note.

15. Cf. M. Gilbert, "Wisdom Literature," in *Jewish Writings of the Second Temple Period: Apocrypha, Pseudepigrapha, Qumran Sectarian Writings, Philo, Josephus* (ed. M. E. Stone; Compendia rerum iudaicarum ad Novum Testamentum 2.2; Assen: Van Gorcum/Philadelphia: Fortress, 1984), 283–324; and R. E. Murphy, *The Tree of Life: An Exploration of Biblical Wisdom Literature* (Anchor Bible Reference Library; New York: Doubleday, 1990).

16. Gilbert, "Wisdom Literature," 290–301.

17. Translations of the Wisdom of Ben Sira are from P. W. Skehan and A. A. Di Lella, *The Wisdom of Ben Sira* (Anchor Bible 39; New York: Doubleday, 1987).

18. This line differs slightly from Skehan and Di Lella's translation ("all this is true of the book of the Most High's covenant") and keeps closer to the Greek text.

19. Translation from J. Goldin, *The Living Talmud: The Wisdom of the Fathers and Its Classical Commentaries* (Chicago: University of Chicago Press, 1957), 43.

20. Translation from E. Cashdan, *Menahoth*, vol. 2 in *The Babylonian Talmud: Seder Kodashim* (I. Epstein; London: Soncino, 1948), 190.

21. There are some other problems in this particular translation, which I cannot deal with here; for instance, it reads, most probably under Christian influence, "the son of God." See A. Diez Macho (ed.), *Neophyti 1* (Madrid/Barcelona: Consejo Superior de Investigaciones Científicas, 1968–74), 1.2–3, 497n. 1, where the translators state that "the word *Memera* . . . is probably missing in the text . . . and therefore one should translate: 'From the beginning (the word) of the Lord with wisdom created and perfected the heavens and the earth.'"

22. This particular homily is called *Petikhah*; cf. Strack and Stemberger, *Introduction to the Talmud and Midrash*, 301–2.

23. New Jewish Publication Society Version has "instruction."

24. Translation from Goldin, *Living Talmud*, 140.

25. Translation from *Mekilta de-Rabbi Ishmael* (trans. J. Z. Lauterbach; Philadelphia: Jewish Publication Society of America, 1949), 2.234–44.

26. Cf. *Genesis Rabbah* 63.14; for further references see L. Ginzberg, *The Legends of the Jews* (Philadelphia: Jewish Publication Society, 1968), 5.277–78, 281–82, 296.

27. Cf. *Genesis Rabbah* 63.7 and Ginzberg, *Legends of the Jews*, 5.116, 271–73, 278, 280, 294, 309.

28. Cf. *Genesis Rabbah* 85.8 and Ginzberg, *Legends of the Jews*, 5.223–34.

29. They belong to the so-called seven Noachide laws considered by the rabbis as applying to all humankind; cf. Babylonian Talmud, tractate *Sanhedrin* 56a.

Chapter 3

The Gospel of John and Philo of Alexandria

Peder Borgen

Let me first characterize the Gospel of John and Philo of Alexandria as I see them. The Gospel of John was written toward the end of the first century C.E. I am among those scholars who think that it draws on traditions that are independent of the three other Gospels, although some of the traditional units used were parallel to some of those found in the other three. In the Gospel of John the traditions are interpreted and applied to new situations. My comparison of the Gospel of John and Philo of Alexandria focuses attention more on these interpretative aspects than on the question of the pre-Johannine stages of the Gospel traditions. Philo of Alexandria was a Jewish exegete who interpreted the laws of Moses on the basis of Jewish exegetical traditions and Greek philosophical ideas. He partly applied his exegesis to his own contemporary situation. Philo lived in Alexandria from about 15 B.C.E. to about 50 C.E. A large number of his treatises have been preserved.[1]

My present task is focused. I shall examine how aspects of Philo's writings, written during the first half of the first century C.E., can illuminate aspects of the Gospel of John, which was written during the last half of the first century C.E. At the outset I shall offer glimpses from British scholar C. H. Dodd's interpretation of the Gospel of John, since to him Philo of Alexandria provided the most important background material for the Gospel. My own work has focused more on John and Philo as exegetes of the Old Testament. In their use of traditions and in their expositions, both John and Philo characterize the people of God, although with different results. Philo saw them as the Jewish people of the synagogue and criticizes some who were in danger of passing the community border. John is situated within a group that had been separated from the synagogal community and that understood itself in continuity and discontinuity with its Jewish heritage. Among the topics to be discussed here are the Sabbath observance, birth from above, the Temple, and ascent and descent.

Dodd's Comparison of John and Philo

According to C. H. Dodd a real affinity existed between Philo and John in their use of symbolism.[2] To Philo a symbol points to a hidden meaning, on the abstract, intellectual level.[3] To John a narrative is at the same time factually true and symbolic of a deeper truth, since things and events in this world derive what reality they possess from the eternal ideas they embody.[4] Some examples can indicate the similarity and the difference between Philo and John in the use of symbolism. Philo can talk about God or Wisdom (Sophia)/the Word (Logos) as the archetype of light (*On Dreams* 1.75). The corresponding Johannine term is the true light (John 1:9).[5]

John speaks of living water and of a spring of water (John 4:10, 14). Philo speaks of the immortal-making well (*On the Special Laws* 1.303; *On Flight and Finding* §§197–99).[6]

Both writers use the symbol of the shepherd.[7] Philo uses it in connection with God: "Indeed, so good a thing is shepherding that it is justly ascribed not to kings only and wise men and perfectly cleansed souls but also to God the All-Sovereign" (*On Agriculture* §50). The authority for this ascription is not any ordinary one but a prophet, whom we do well to trust. This is the way in which the psalmist speaks: "The Lord shepherds me and nothing shall be lacking to me" (Psalms 23:1; see further *On the Posterity of Cain* §§67–68). John sees Christ as the shepherd (John 10:1–18, 25–29).

For both, to know God is the chief end of humankind and its highest blessedness. Philo says, "All flesh has corrupted the perfect way of the eternal and incorruptible which leads to God. This way is wisdom, for led by this straight and level way reason arrives at the goal; and the goal of the way is knowledge and recognition of God" (*That God Is Unchangeable* §§142–43).[8] Compare with this John 14:6: "I am the way," and 17:3: "And this is eternal life, that they know you the only God, and Jesus Christ whom you have sent."

Besides such more abstract and mystical concepts, Philo also can touch thoughts of a more personal relationship to God — as worship and the concepts of faith and love. In the Gospel of John faith and love are central thoughts.[9]

For Philo, God was transcendent and could not be identified with the world or any part of it. Platonic and Stoic ideas helped him to express the relationship between God and the world. Here the Word is the Mediator. The Word proceeds from God and is the medium of the creation of the world. The higher, intelligible world cannot be thought of in terms of space, but it is the Word of God in the act of creating the world (*On the Creation of the World* §§16–24).[10]

The Word (Logos) is also the medium of the divine government of the world.[11] It is not only transcendent in the mind of God, but also immanent in the created universe (*On the Cherubim* §36; *That God Is Unchangeable* §57; *On Agriculture* §51; etc.). Dodd concludes, "In all respects the Logos is the medium of intercourse between God and this world."[12]

By the Word, Logos, then, Philo means the Platonic world of ideas, conceived not as self-existent, but as expressing the mind of the One God. We find in the prologue of John parallels of Philo's thoughts about the Word and world, creation, government, and communication.

Dodd was aware that similar ideas were associated with the Jewish concept of wisdom. He therefore examined Wisdom literature and tabulated an extensive list of parallels.[13] With the concept of wisdom, Dodd believed that "we are already half-way to Philo's Logos."[14] And it was in Philo that he found the material to supplement the Old Testament so as to explain John's understanding of the Word (Logos), which was not simply the uttered word of God, but implied the ideas of plan and purpose. Dodd concluded that "any reader influenced by the thought of Hellenistic Judaism, directly or at a remove, would inevitably find suggested here [in John's prologue] a conception of the creative and revealing [Logos] in many respects similar to that of Philo; and it is difficult not to think that the author intended this."[15]

Use of Scripture: Genesis 1:1–3

My approach will differ somewhat from that of Dodd's. He places emphasis on similar ideas and outlook. More attention needs to be given to the use of the Old Testament by Philo and John and to the situation of the Johannine community reflected in the Gospel. As for the use of the Old Testament, already the prologue of John makes evident that this question is important, since John 1:1 ("in the beginning was the Word") clearly refers to the story of the creation, in particular to Genesis 1:1 ("in the beginning God created").[16]

The opening Greek phrase, which in English translation reads "in the beginning," is identical with the Septuagint translation of Genesis 1:1 into Greek. Thus one should consider the possibility that the Greek text of 1:3 formed the background of the term *the Word* (Logos): "And God said, 'Let there be light.' " German scholar E. Haenchen objects to this explanation of the term Logos. He maintains that nowhere in Jewish sources is the phrase *and God said* interpreted as a personalized Word distinct from God.[17] Haenchen overlooks that Philo's understanding of "and God said" in 1:3 does not mean merely the spoken word but refers to the Word (Logos) as the model, the paradigm (*On Dreams* 1.75).[18] Moreover, in *On the Confusion of Tongues* §146, alluding to points from the creation story and other passages in the Old Testament, Philo pictures Logos as a personified figure "under God's First-born, Logos, the oldest of the angels, as the Archangel. He has many names, for he is called 'the Beginning' and 'the Name of God' and 'Logos' and 'the Man after His image' and 'he that sees,' Israel."[19] When the Archangel is called "the Beginning," it is a personification of the word *beginning* in Genesis 1:1; "Logos" is then a personification of 1:3, "God said." "The Man after his [God's] image" comes from 1:26, "Let us make man according to our image," here interpreted to mean the Archangel and not created humans. Thus, Philo demonstrates that the phrase *God said* in 1:3 is seen as an entity distinct from God and even personified as an archangel. There is good reason, therefore, for regarding the Word (Logos) of John's prologue as an elaboration of Genesis 1:3, "God said."[20]

What about the idea of (God's) Wisdom as the background idea for the Johannine Logos? This suggestion receives support from Philo, since he relates Wisdom to creation in a way similar to his elaborations on the Word. His interpretation of Wisdom demonstrates the importance of this term's feminine gender, however. In *On Drunkenness* §§30–31 Philo refers to the role of Wisdom in creation, citing Proverbs 8:22. He spells out the female aspect of Wisdom, Sophia, and the synonymous feminine Greek word *epistēmē* (knowledge). Philo sees God as the Father of creation, Sophia as the Mother, and creation itself as the birth of the visible world, the only beloved son which we see:

The Demiurge who made this universe was at the same time the
father of what was thus born, while its mother was the Knowledge (*epistēmēn*) possessed by its Maker. With his Knowledge
God had union, not as men have it, and begat created being.
And Knowledge, having received the divine seed, when her
travail was consummated bore the only beloved Son who is
apprehended by the senses, the world which we see. Thus in
the pages of one of the inspired company, Wisdom (*sophia*) is
represented as speaking of herself after this manner: "God obtained me first of all his works and founded me before the ages"
(Proverbs 8:22).[21]

Philo's interpretation of the role of Wisdom (*sophia*)
and Knowledge (*epistēmē*) in creation supports the view that
John's prologue is influenced by Jewish ideas about the personified Wisdom's role in creation (*On Drunkenness* §§30–31).
However, Philo's exploitation of the feminine gender of Wisdom and Knowledge to mean that she was God's female
partner and Mother of the visible world demonstrates the
difficulty in identifying a male figure, such as Jesus Christ,
by these feminine terms. Thus, there were good reasons for
using the masculine term *logos* in John's prologue and not
the feminine word *sophia*.

Use of Scripture: Genesis 2:2–3

In John 5:1–18 Jesus healed an invalid at the Beth-zatha pool.
When it is said in 5:17 that God works up to now — that is,
including the Sabbath — a widespread Jewish exegetical debate on Genesis 2:2–3, that God rested on the seventh day, is
presupposed and used.[22] The problem was the conviction that
God cannot stop working in the upholding of the world. Consequently, the notion of the Sabbath rest of God, as stated in
2:2–3 (God rested on the seventh day), stands in tension with
this working. Evidence for such exegetical debate on the Sabbath rest of God is found as early as the second century B.C.E.
in writings of Jewish Alexandrian exegete Aristobulus,[23] and
more material is found in Philo and in other Jewish (rabbinic)

writings.[24] Philo, relying on the Septuagint rendering, notices that 2:2–3 has a Greek word that he understands to mean "put down/cause to rest," and not the related Greek word that means "to rest." Philo interprets 2:2–3 in this way: "For he causes to rest that which, though actually not in operation, is apparently making, but he himself never ceases making" (*Allegorical Interpretation* 1.5–6). Thus, the meaning of the seventh day to Philo is that God, who has no origin, is always active. "He is not a mere artificer, but also Father of the things that are coming into being" (*Allegorical Interpretation* 1.18). All created beings are dependent and really inactive in all their doings: "The seventh day is meant to teach the power of the Unoriginate and the non-action of created beings" (*On the Migration of Abraham* §91).

An interpretation of Genesis 2:2–3 similar to that of Philo's seems to be presupposed in John 5:1–18. The Son of God brings the Father's upholding and providential activity to bear upon the case of the healing of a person on the Sabbath. And the healed person is dependent and inactive, even in the carrying of the mat on the Sabbath, because the Son of God told him to do so. Jesus said: "My Father is working still, and I am working" (5:17).

Use of Scripture: Bread from Heaven

Dialogue

Another exposition of scripture produces much material for comparison of John and Philo; that is, the exposition of the giving of manna in John 6. Only a few salient points can be discussed here.

John 6:31 quotes the Old Testament: "Bread from heaven he gave them to eat."[25] This quotation is interpreted by means of a paraphrase in 6:31–58. The setting is pictured as one in which dialogues take place, a dialogue between "they" (i.e., the crowd) and Jesus (6:28–40), which prompts reactions

and objections among the Jews in a dialogue with Jesus
(6:41–58).

In John 6:59 Jesus spoke in a synagogue, as he taught
at Capernaum. British scholar C. K. Barrett comments: "At
v. 24 we learned that the scene was Capernaum, but the
discourse with its interruptions suggests a less formal occasion than a synagogue sermon."[26] Against Barrett, it must be
said that interruptions in the form of questions and answers,
direct exegesis, and problem-solving exegesis were part of
the discourses at the synagogal gatherings. All of these elements are found in rabbinic exegetical elaborations called
midrashim, for example, the commentary *Mekilta* on Exodus
and Philo's commentaries. A glimpse into such practice is
given by Philo in his description of the Therapeutai. When
they assemble, the leader "examines (seeks) some points in
the sacred writings, or also solves that which is propounded
by another" (*On the Contemplative Life* §75). The term *examine* (*zēteō* and the composite verb *epizēteō*) are used elsewhere
in Philo's writings when an exegetical question is raised,
such as in *On the Creation of the World* §77: "One might examine (*epizētēseie*) the reason because of which..." (cf. *On the
Special Laws* 1.214; *Allegorical Interpretation* 1.33, 48, 91; 2.103;
and *Questions and Answers on Genesis* 1.62 [Greek fragment]).
Answers and solutions are given, and in *Allegorical Interpretation* 3.60 the verb *lyō* (to solve) is used, corresponding to
the use of the composite verb *epilyō* in *On the Contemplative
Life* §75: "The leader 'examines (*zētei*) some points in the
sacred writings, or also solves (*epilyetai*) that which is propounded by another.'" In *On the Contemplative Life* §79 the
leader is said to have discoursed (*dieilechthai*), and since questions and answers were part of the discourse, the verb means
"to discuss."[27]

Against this background the following conclusion can
be drawn: in John 6:30 ("what sign do you do?") John re-
counts an incident from the Gospel tradition where Jesus was
asked to give a sign and then gave his answer (see John 2:18;
Matthew 16:1–4/Mark 8:11–13; cf. Matthew 21:23–27/Mark

11:27–33/Luke 20:1–8). When John elaborates upon this and various Gospel traditions in 6:30–58, he develops the exegesis of an Old Testament quotation in a dialogue, a method and form also exemplified by Philo. Thus, the reference to a synagogal setting in 6:59 is appropriate.

Exegetical Exchange

The dialogue may include objections and replies.[28] This form should be examined further in John 6. The Jews' objection to Jesus' exegesis of manna in 6:41–42 is expressed by a term from the story about manna in Exodus 16:2, 7, 8: "murmured" (John 6:41, 43). The objection has the form of an exegetical problem formulation followed by a solution, parallels to which are found in Philo. The exposition consists of the following points:

1. The Old Testament quotation: "Bread from heaven he gave them to eat" (John 6:31).

2. The interpretation of the quotation, citing words in John 6:35, 38: "He [Jesus] said, '*I am the bread which came down from heaven*'" (6:41).

3. The basis for the questioning of Jesus' exegesis: "They said, 'Is not this Jesus, the son of Joseph, whose father and mother we know?' " (John 6:42).

4. The questioning of the interpretation: "How does he now say, '*I have come down from heaven*'?" (John 6:42).

5. The answer to the objection and the solution of the problem: "Jesus answered and said to them, 'Do not "murmur" among yourselves' " (John 6:43–51).[29]

In my book *Bread from Heaven*, I refer to the corresponding points of exegetical exchange found in the Jewish commentary *Mekilta* on Exodus 12:1–2 and in Philo's *On the Change of Names* §§141–44.[30] The Philonic passage is relevant to our discussion here:[31]

1. The Old Testament quotation (Genesis 17:16): "So much for the phrase 'I will give to you.' We must now explain 'from her'" (§141).
2. The interpretation of the quotation in which "from her" is rendered "the mother": "There is a third class who say that virtue is *the mother* of any good that has come into being, receiving the seeds from nothing that is mortal" (§142).
3. The basis for questioning the interpretation: "Some ask, however, whether the barren can bear children, since the oracles earlier describe Sarah as barren" (§143).
4. The questioning of the interpretation: "And now admit that she will become *a mother*" (§143).
5. The answer to the objection and the solution of the problem: "Our answer to this must be that it is not the nature of a barren woman to bear, any more than of the blind to see or of the deaf to hear. But as for the soul which is sterilized to wickedness and unfruitful of the endless host of passions and vices, scarce any prosper in childbirth as she. For she bears offspring worthy of love, even the number seven.... The mind ... holds fast to the 'seventh' and the supreme peace which it gives. This peace she would fain bear in her womb and be called its *mother*" (§§143–44).

Philological Exegesis

Philological exegesis is part of John's exposition in John 6: 31–32:[32]

1. The Old Testament quotation: *"Bread from heaven he gave them to eat"* (John 6:31).
2. Exposition: "Jesus then said to them, 'It was not Moses who gave (Hebrew *natan*) you *the bread from heaven;*

my Father *gives* (Hebrew *noten*) you *the* true *bread from heaven'* " (John 6:32).

Here words in and from the Old Testament quotation (indicated by italic type) are woven together with other words. Moreover, the different tenses of *gave* and *gives* are due to different vocalizations of the Hebrew word behind the Greek text: *natan* (gave) and *noten* (gives). Similar methods and forms are found in the Jewish exegetical commentaries, the *midrashim*, and in Philo.[33]

Other Points of Similarity

Although the exposition in John 6:31–58 consists of dialogue including scholarly exchanges, several unifying threads demonstrate that the passage is composed as a whole: The statement *our fathers ate manna in the wilderness* in 6:31 is repeated with some changes in 6:49, 58. Even more important, throughout the section the words *bread from heaven he gave them* (6:31) are built into the formulations, and in 6:49–58 the remaining word in the Old Testament quotation in 6:31, "to eat," is added. These threads, which run through 6:31–58, show that the passage is in a systematic way constructed as a homiletic whole.

Philo offers many examples of exegetical paraphrase in which an Old testament quotation is interpreted in a systematic way. *Allegorical Interpretation* 3.162–68 serves as an example, paraphrasing and discussing Exodus 16:4, quoted as text in §162a:

a. Behold I rain upon you bread out of heaven.

b. And the people shall go out and they shall gather the day's portion for a day.

c. That I may prove them whether they will walk by my law or not.[34]

Conflicts and Punishments

Sabbath Controversy

Philo can even throw light upon John beyond the area of exegetical methods and exegetical traditions. His writings illustrate how exegesis of the laws of Moses played a role in controversies in the Jewish community. He provides comparative material to the way in which exegesis of the laws of Moses, *in casu* Genesis 2:2–3 in John 5:1–18, was a factor in the controversy between the synagogue and the emerging Christian community. Let us elaborate a little further on this topic here, drawing on additional material from Philo's writings.

According to John 5:1–18 God's providential activity was made manifest in the healing of the paralytic by the Son on the Sabbath. On the basis of God's/the Son's work on the Sabbath, Sabbath observances could be abrogated. Jesus' healing of the man therefore caused a conflict to arise.[35] Against this background it is of special interest to note that in *On the Migration of Abraham* §§91–93 Philo gives the following advice and warning against those who draw wrong conclusions from the circumstance that God is active on the seventh day, as stated in Genesis 2:2–3 according to Jewish exegesis:

> It is quite true that the seventh day is meant to teach the power of the Unorginate and the non-action of created beings (cf. Genesis 2:2–3). But let us not for this reason abrogate (*lyōmen*) the enactments laid down for its observance, and light fires or till the ground or carry loads or institute proceedings in court or act as jurors or demand the restoration of deposits or recover loans, or do all else that we are permitted to do as well on days that are not festival seasons.... Why, we shall be ignoring the sanctity of the Temple and a thousand other things, if we are going to pay heed to nothing except what is shown us by the inner meaning of things. Nay, we should look on all these outward observances as resembling the body, and their inner meanings as resembling the soul,... so we must pay heed to the letter of the laws. If we keep and observe these, we shall gain a clearer conception of those things of which these are the

symbols; and besides that we shall not incur the censure of the many and the charges they are sure to bring against us.

Here we find a conflict between two ways of reasoning, both relying upon the laws of Moses. Philo's view might be characterized in this way: the universal principles and activity of the Creator are tied to the external observances of a particular people, the Jewish nation. The view that Philo criticizes seems to be that the laws of Moses and the specific observances give witness to the universal principles and activity of the Creator. The universal principles can then be followed by those who hold on to them even apart from the particular external observances. Consequently, God's activity and universal principles can be present also when one works and is active in society at large on the Sabbath, just as one does on other days.

On the Migration of Abraham §§91–93 also has points of similarities with John 5:1–18. In both places the exegesis of Genesis 2:2–3 is presupposed and used, although this Old Testament passage is not quoted and therefore not interpreted in an explicit way. In both places the scripture is applied to specific controversies related to Sabbath observance. The Sabbath gives witness to the understanding that God is always active. This understanding is what matters. Thus there is freedom as to the specific observances, such as the prohibition against carrying a load.

In John 5:10–12 the load is the mat carried by the one healed. Also the criticism of Jesus' healing on the Sabbath is in accordance with *On the Migration of Abraham* §§91–93, when Philo prohibits such actions that could be done just as easily on days other than on the festival seasons. There is a basic difference, however, between the spiritualizing Jews whom Philo criticizes and the views expressed in John. According to John, the activity of the Creator is the basis of the activity of the Son on the Sabbath, and the Son is the historical person Jesus of Nazareth. This view leads to the conclusion that the Sabbath observances against healing and against the carrying of a load could be set aside. The spiritualists in Alexandria, on the other hand, referred to an idea and a doctrine of God's providential activity in defense of their freedom from Sabbath observances.

Informer or Witness?

Further discussion is needed on the life-setting of the passage (John 5:1–18) in John's community. American scholar J. L. Martyn thinks that the passage reflects a certain historical incident in the life of the Johannine church: a member of John's church serves to make real in the life of a Jew the healing power of Jesus. At that, the Jewish authorities step in and question the man. Then the Christian finds the man and talks with him, but does not lead him to full Christian confession. He rather gives him a solemn warning as stated in 5:14: "See, you are well! Sin no more, that nothing worse befall you." The man represents the Jew who, though presumably thankful to be healed, nevertheless remains wholly loyal to the synagogue and even becomes an informer against his healer.[36] In support of his interpretation Martyn points to the parallelism between 5:15 ("the man went away and told the Jews that it was Jesus who had healed him") and 11:46 ("but some of them went to the Pharisees and told them what Jesus had done").[37]

Against this understanding of Martyn, I stress the basic difference between the two statements. In John 5:15 *the man healed* by Jesus (and not some spectators) tells the Jewish authorities who healed him. In 11:46 *the spectators* to Jesus' calling Lazarus back from the grave reported it to the Pharisees. The healing story in 5:1–18 is, rather, an initiation story that serves as a paradigm for entry into the Johannine community. The healing represents salvation as a whole, and 5:14 ("See you are well! Sin no more, that nothing worse befall you")[38] is an admonition to a convert to live a new life.

When the man went away and told the Jewish authorities that Jesus had healed him (John 5:15), he gave his witness to them about Jesus as his healer. This open information to the Jewish authorities about the healing incident is in general agreement with the point made in 18:20 that Jesus said nothing secretly.

Discontinuity and Continuity

Dangers at the Boundary

Those whom Philo criticizes and warns about abrogating the observance of the Sabbath and other observances in *On the Migration of Abraham* §§91–93 were in danger of crossing the boundary away from the synagogal community and thus of being subject to censure and accusations.

When the Jewish exegesis of Genesis 2:2–3 of God's working on the Sabbath is applied in John 5:1–18 to Jesus and his healing activity on the Sabbath, it leads to the charge by the Jewish leaders that he did not only break the Sabbath, but also made himself equal to God. For this reason the Jewish authorities sought to kill him (cf. 5:18). They understood Jesus' claim to mean ditheism, which qualified for the death penalty. According to 16:2–3 the disciples also might be killed: "The hour is coming when whoever kills you will think he is offering service to God. And they will do this because they have not known the Father, nor me."

Martyn and others here refer to Deuteronomy 13 as a probable judicial basis, according to which enticement to serve other gods is a crime that brings the death penalty. This understanding receives support from Philo, who has a paraphrased rendering of Deuteronomy 13 in *On the Special Laws* 1.315–18. He applies the passage to the situation when a person who claims to be an inspired prophet leads people to worship the gods recognized in the different cities. Several points of similarity are found between this passage in Philo and John: (1) the ones who commit the crime claim divine legitimation, as inspired prophet (Philo) or Jesus as the

Son of God (John); (2) the crime is that of partaking in polytheism (Philo) or ditheism (John); (3) the death penalty may
be executed without regular court procedure being followed
(not explicitly stated in Deuteronomy 13); and (4) the killing
is seen as a service to God.

One difference is that Philo elaborates on the point in
Deuteronomy 13 about polytheism in a pagan city, while
the problem in John is the claim of a fellow Jew, Jesus,
which is understood to mean ditheism. Since ditheism is
one form of polytheism, it is probable that John presupposes
juridical traditions that draw on Deuteronomy 13. Philo's
paraphrasing interpretation of this text demonstrates that in
contemporary Judaism some advocated the death penalty for
Jews who accepted polytheistic views and practices, and they
even sharpened Deuteronomy 13 to mean execution without
proper trial.

Birth from Above

Barrett suggests that the point of departure for the evolu-
tion of the terminology *birth from above* is primarily the Jesus
logion about the need for becoming like children in order
to enter the kingdom (cf. Matthew 18:3 and parallels). The
belief that the kingdom was not only to be expected in the
age to come but has already been manifested, germinally or
potentially, in the person and work of Jesus distinguished
earliest Christianity from Judaism and made possible the
development of the traditional material in Hellenistic terminology, where rebirth and supernatural begetting were not
uncommon. John did not plagiarize the notions of salvation
and regeneration current in the Hellenistic world or effect a
syncretism of Jewish and pagan ideas. According to Barrett,
he perceived that the language of Judaism ("the kingdom of
God") and the language of Hellenism ("birth from above")
provided him with a unique opportunity of expressing what
was neither Jewish nor Hellenistic but simply Christian.[39]

There are, however, exegetical traditions that give basis for placing John's idea of rebirth within a Jewish setting. Thus, Philo says in *Questions and Answers on Exodus* 2.46 that Moses' ascent at Sinai was a second birth, different from the first. Philo interprets Exodus 24:16: "The glory of the Lord settled on Mount Sinai, and the cloud covered it six days; and on the seventh day he called to Moses out of the midst of the cloud." Philo interprets God's calling of Moses on the seventh day:

> But the calling above of the prophet is a second birth better than the first. For the latter is mixed with a body and had corruptible parents, while the former is an unmixed and simple soul of the sovereign, being changed from a productive to an unproductive form, which has no mother but only a father, who is (the Father) of all. Wherefore, the "calling above" or, as we have said, the divine birth happened to come about for him in accordance with the ever-virginal nature of the hebdomad. For he "is called on the seventh day," in this (respect) differing from the earthborn first moulded man, for the latter came into being from the earth and with a body, while the former (came) from ether and without a body. Wherefore the most appropriate number, six, was assigned to the earth-born man, while to the one differently born (was assigned) the higher nature of the hebdomad.

There are several agreements between the Philonic passage and John 3:3–15 and 1:13:[40] (a) the idea of birth (3:5; 1:13); (b) this birth is from above (3:3–15; Philo: "calling above" = "from ether"); (c) it is a birth with God as father, without a mother (1:13); (d) it is a second birth, different from birth from a woman (3:3–8); (e) John's distinction between "flesh" and "spirit" corresponds to Philo's "body" and "mind."[41]

Moses' rebirth is in Philo identified with Moses' experience at Sinai. The implication is that Philo draws on Jewish exegetical traditions that he develops further in his interpretation. This understanding is supported by the interpretation of the experience of the burning bush and the revelation at Sinai as birth in Jewish (rabbinic) traditions, as E. Stein and E. Sjäberg show.[42] Sjäberg gives the exegetical commentary *Song of Songs Rabbah* 8.2 as an example:

" 'I would lead you, and bring you' (Song of Songs 8:2): I would lead you from the upper world to the lower. 'I would bring you into my mother's house' (Song of Songs 8:2): this is Sinai. R. Berekiah said: Why is Sinai called 'my mother's house' (Song of Songs 8:2)? Because there Israel became like a newborn child."[43]

Sjäberg states that according to Rabbi Berekiah the Israelites at Sinai came into a completely new situation. Their relationship to God was rebuilt upon a completely new foundation. Rabbi Berekiah's word about Israel as a newborn child was an interpretation of the "mother" mentioned in *Song of Songs Rabbah* 8.2, and it is therefore evident that the picture of birth is meant here. Other parallels exist, such as in the Jewish exegetical commentary *Exodus Rabbah* 30.5, which says that the Law, the Torah, conceived Israel at Sinai.

Stein draws attention to *Exodus Rabbah* 3.15 on Exodus 4:12 and the Jewish exegetical commentary *Tanhuma, Shemoth* 18, about Moses' vision of the burning bush.[44] According to this piece of tradition, God's relationship to Moses was compared with that of a mother who conceives and gives birth to a child, when God dedicated Moses and commissioned him to his high charge.[45] Moses at the burning bush experienced rebirth.[46]

Although the dates of the written forms of *Songs of Songs Rabbah, Exodus Rabbah,* and *Tanhuma* are late, these passages and Philo's *Questions and Answers on Exodus* 2.46 illuminate each other. The rabbinic passages support the hypothesis that Philo relies on Jewish exegesis as the basis for his understanding of the Sinaitic ascent as rebirth, and Philo supports the hypothesis that the core of the later rabbinic passages goes back to the beginning of the first century or earlier.

The conclusion is that we have a basis for interpreting birth from above in John 1:13 and 3:3–15 against the background of Moses' and Israel's rebirth at the Sinai event and at the burning bush incident. This concept of rebirth is then in John combined with the word from the Gospel tradition about being like a child as condition for entry into heaven. This understanding of 3:3–15 makes Jesus' rebuke of Nicodemus the point: "Are you the teacher of Israel, and yet you do not understand this?" The idea of discontinuity and new beginning associated with the Sinai event is in John transferred to the new beginning in the life and teachings of Jesus, the incarnate one. Thus Nicodemus had to face the message of discontinuity with his own background as "the teacher of Israel" as the condition for seeing/entering the kingdom of God. John has transferred Sinaitic traditions about birth to mean the birth of the people of God who believed in Jesus as the Son of God.[47] Understandably then 3:11 reflects the experience of the Johannine community by plural *we:* "We are talking about what we know, and we are testifying to what we have seen; but you people do not accept our testimony."

The Temple

At times Philo personifies the Jerusalem Temple by seemingly transferring it to the religious life of individuals. Thus the external Temple and the actual city of Jerusalem seem to be of no value: "Do not seek for the city of the Existent among the regions of the earth, since it is not wrought of wood and stone, but in a soul, in which there is no warring. . . . For what grander or holier house could we find for God in the whole range of existence than the vision-seeking mind?" (*On Dreams* 2.250–51).

Similarly, in *On the Cherubim* §§98–107 the main theme is that the house prepared for God the King of kings, the Lord of all, is not made of stone and timber, but it is the soul that is fitted to him. In the invisible soul the invisible God has his earthly dwelling place. To this temple belongs teaching, virtues, and noble actions.[48]

Philo does not in this way ignore the earthly Temple made by hands, however, but the spiritual and personal appropriation is seen as basic. Accordingly he warns the spiritualists in *On the Migration of Abraham* §§91–93 that "we shall be ignoring the sanctity of the Temple and a thousand other things, if we are going to pay heed to nothing except what is shown us by the inner meaning of things.... As we have to take thought for the body, because it is the abode of the soul, so we must pay heed to the letter of the laws."

The Temple is also personified in John's Gospel, here exclusively applied to one person, Jesus Christ, the incarnate Word, Logos. Jesus is the divine tabernacle (1:14): "And the Word became flesh and tabernacled among us." His person ("body") in life, death, and resurrection is the temple (2:19–22): "Jesus answered them, 'Destroy this temple, and in three days I will raise it up.' The Jews then said, 'It has taken forty-six years to build this temple, and will you raise it up in three days?' But he spoke of the temple of his body. When therefore he was raised from the dead, his disciples remembered that he had said this."

Jesus' appearances and teaching activity at the feasts in and outside of the Temple, such as at Sabbath, Passover, Tabernacles, and Dedication, interpret their meaning and replace their significance.[49] In this way the true Temple has been transferred onto Jesus Christ in whom the disciples, including the members of the Johannine community, believe. Here also the Johannine community formulates and applies the continuity with the biblical-Jewish traditions in such a way that it means discontinuity with the synagogal community. Thus the Johannine community went further than those whom Philo criticizes. They were warned not to pass the boundary away from the practicing Jewish community around Temple and synagogue, while the Johannine community had experienced a traumatic separation away from it.[50]

Ascent and Descent

Only a few observations on the theme of ascent and descent in Philo and John can be dealt with in this study.

In the biblical story about the Sinaitic revelation the term *ascend* plays a central role (cf. Exodus 19:20, 23; 24:1,

2, 9, 13, 18). In Jewish exegesis it can be said that Moses entered into heaven when he ascended. This view is quite widespread (Philo, *On the Life of Moses* 1.158–59; cf. Josephus, *Jewish Antiquities* 3.96; Pseudo-Philo [*Biblical Antiquities*] 12.1; *Mekilta* on Exodus 19:20; *Numbers Rabbah* 12.11; *Midrash on the Psalms* 24.5; 106.2). John 3:13, "No one has ascended to heaven," seems then to serve as a polemic both against the idea of Moses' ascent and against similar claims of or for other human beings. Philo gives an explicit formulation of this idea of *imitatio Mosis* in *On the Life of Moses* 1.158. After having told about Moses' entry into the place where God was, he concluded, "He has set before us...a model for those who are willing to copy it."[51] As an example of a claim made by another human being, one might refer to Philo's own ascent to the heavenly sphere: "I...seemed always to be borne aloft into the heights with a soul possessed by some God-sent inspiration" (*On the Special Laws* 3.1–6).[52] John 3:13 is probably a polemic against persons in the Johannine environment who maintained that they were visionaries like Moses.[53] Thus, John's Gospel reflects an environment like that exemplified by Philo, in which Jewish versions of ascent traditions existed and persons experienced heavenly ascents in the Spirit.

This Johannine polemic is partly due to the conviction that what is to be sought in heaven, such as God's glory, is now in the incarnate one present on earth. Thus the ascent motif is put upside down in John's Gospel when it is applied to the incarnate Logos/Son. Several examples of such a descent motif are found in Philo's writings.[54]

Agent: "He Who Is Sent"

A frequently used characterization of Jesus in John is "the one who is sent by the Father"[55] and similar phrases, and Jesus characterizes God as "the one who sent me" and similar phrases: "And he who sees me sees Him who sent me" (12:45). God the Father sent the Son, and the Son sent his disciples: "As you sent me into the world, so I have sent them into the world" (17:18). Thus, John applies ideas of agency and diplomacy to Christology.

The technical Greek term for an envoy, *presbeutēs*, is applied by Philo to human envoys. Flaccus answered the Alexandrian Jews who asked him to forward their decree to the Roman Emperor Gaius: "I will send it [the decree] as you ask or will fulfill the duties of an envoy (*presbeutēs*) myself that Gaius may learn your gratitude" (*Against Flaccus* §98). As the leader of the Jewish delegation/envoys to the Emperor Gaius in Rome, Philo was alarmed by the emperor's seemingly goodwill and said: "Why when so many envoys (*presbeutōn*) were present from almost the whole world did he say that he would hear us only?" (*On the Embassy to Gaius* §182). Philo later writes, "Surely it was a cruel situation that the fate of all the Jews everywhere should rest precariously on us five envoys (*presbeutais*)" (§370).

Philo also uses this idea of envoys on the spiritual and divine level. He calls the personified Word/Logos an envoy. Logos acts as ambassador of the ruler, God, to his subjects: "This same Logos both pleads with the immortal as suppliant for afflicted mortality and acts as ambassador (*presbeutēs*) of the ruler to the subject" (*Who Is the Heir?* §205). The term is, furthermore, used by Philo about angels who are envoys backward and forward between humans and God (*On Giants* §16). Angels are "the servitors and lieutenants of the primal God whom he employs as ambassadors to announce the predictions which he wills to make to our [Jewish] race" (*On the Life of Abraham* §115). Here the notions of ascent and descent are evident. Thus Philo exemplifies a kind of Jewish milieu that serves as background for John's elaborations on the Jesus logion about God as the sender and Jesus as the one who is sent.[56]

Wisdom: The Law and Manna

In John 6:31–58 Jesus identifies himself with the bread from heaven, which like the law of Moses gives life to the world[57] and which like Wisdom satisfies the thirst and hunger of those who come:

> Jesus then said to them, "Truly, truly, I say to you, it was not Moses who gave you the bread from heaven; my Father gives you the true bread from heaven. For the bread of God is that which comes down from heaven and gives life to the world." They said to him, "Lord, give us this bread always." Jesus said to them, "I am the bread of life; he who comes to me shall not hunger, and he who believes in me shall never thirst." (John 6:32–35)

In a corresponding way Philo combines wisdom, the Law, and manna in *On the Change of Names* §§253–63, where it is said that manna that rains down from heaven and is the heavenly Sophia/Wisdom, which is in particular sent from above on the seventh day, on the Sabbath, when the laws of Moses are read and expounded.[58] Important background material is also found in other Jewish writings: "The voice ... gave life to Israel who accepted the Law" (*Tanhuma*, Shemoth 25); "God said to Moses, 'Say to Israel: the Words of the Law which I have given to you ... are life unto you'" (*Mekilta* on Exodus 15:26); "if the earth trembled when he [God] gave life to the world" (*Exodus Rabbah* 29.9).

Again, traditions from and about Jesus have been elaborated upon by the help of biblical and Jewish traditions. In this way the Gospel functioned as a living entity in the life of the Johannine community.

Moses

In Philo's writings Moses is often associated with ascent and, less seldom, descent. Both motifs are present in *On the Sacrifices of Abel and Cain* §§8–9.[59] According to §8 God advanced Moses so high as to place him beside himself, saying to him "stand here with me" (Deuteronomy 5:31). Moses even shared God's nature and was so perfect that he was not "added" at his death (§§8–10). Then in §9 Philo writes:

When he [God] after having lent him to the earthly things, per-
mitted him to associate with them, he endowed him not at all
with some ordinary virtue of a ruler or a king, with which
forcibly to rule the soul's passions, but he appointed him to
be god, having declared the whole bodily realm and its leader,
mind, [to be his] subjects and slaves. "For I give you," he says,
"as god to Pharaoh" (Exodus 7:1).

Correspondingly, Jesus was a divine person who, having
been with God (John 1:1; 17:5) and having been given power
over all flesh (17:2), dwelled among human beings on earth
(1:14; 17:1). While Moses was adopted into his role, Jesus had
been with the Father before the world was made (17:5; cf.
1:1).[60]

When Philo saw Moses placed next to God and appointed
god, then he had to face the problem of whether there were
two gods, ditheism, with regard to Moses, corresponding to
what John faced in his Christology. In different ways both
solved the problem by emphasizing that Moses and Jesus,
respectively, were totally dependent on God. Thus, in *The
Worse Attacks the Better* §§160–61, Philo makes clear that God
is himself true being and active, while Moses was passive
when he appeared and functioned as god, as seen from the
biblical formulation that God *gave him* as "god to Pharaoh"
(Exodus 7:1).

Correspondingly, John placed emphasis on Jesus' func-
tional union with God. In John 10:31–36 Jesus was accused
of blasphemy because he, being a man, made himself God:
"The Jews took up stones again to stone him. Jesus answered
them, 'I have shown you many good works from the Father.
For which of these do you stone me?' The Jews answered
him, 'We stone you for no good work but for blasphemy, because you, being a man, make yourself God.'" Jesus answers
in 10:37–38 that in his works he is in complete union with
his Father: "If I am not doing the works of my Father, then do
not believe in me; but if I do them . . . , believe the works, that
you may know and understand that the Father is in me and I
am in the Father." Thus Jesus did nothing by himself (8:28).

Conclusions

1. Philo demonstrates that the phrase *God said* in Genesis 1:3 is seen as an entity distinct from God and that the Word/Logos is personified as an archangel. There is good reason to regard the Logos of John's prologue as an elaboration of "God said" in Genesis 1:3.

2. The meaning of the seventh day to Philo is that God, who has no origin, is always active, and that he caused his creation to rest on the seventh day, according to Genesis 2:2–3. An interpretation of 2:2–3 similar to that of Philo's seems to be presupposed in John 5:1–18 (the story about the healing of the paralytic) when Jesus says, "My Father is working still, and I am working" (5:17).

3. When John in 6:30–58 develops the exegesis of the Old Testament quotation *bread from heaven he gave them to eat* in the form of a dialogue, he uses a method also exemplified by Philo. Thus, the reference to a synagogal setting in 6:59 is appropriate. Philological exegesis is part of John's exposition, as seen from 6:31–32, where he rejects the reading "gave" (*natan*) in the Old Testament quotation and reads present tense "gives" (*noten*). Similar philological exegesis is found in Philo's writings.

4. Philo criticizes fellow Jews who wanted to abrogate external observances such as the keeping of the Sabbath. Thus, he exemplifies the way in which exegesis of Genesis 2:2–3 in John 5:1–18 was applied to the controversy about the Sabbath; namely, that God also was active on the Sabbath, the day of rest. However, the healing story in 5:1–18 is not only a controversy about the Sabbath. It seems also to be an initiation story that served as a paradigm for entry into the Johannine community.

5. Philo's paraphrasing interpretation of Deuteronomy 13 demonstrates that some in contemporary Judaism advocated the death penalty for Jews who accepted polytheistic views and practices. Philo even sharpened Deuteronomy 13 to mean an execution without proper trial.

Thus Philo illuminates John 16:2: "The hour is coming when whoever kills you will think he is offering service to God."

6. Exegetical traditions give a basis for placing John's idea of rebirth within a Jewish setting, since Philo says in *Questions and Answers on Exodus* 2.46 that Moses' ascent at Sinai was a second birth.

7. At times Philo personifies the Jerusalem Temple by seemingly transferring it to the religious life of persons. There is also a personification of the Temple in John's Gospel, here exclusively applied to one person, Jesus Christ, the incarnate Logos.

8. John 3:13 is probably a polemic against persons in the Johannine environment who maintained that they were visionaries who ascended to heaven like Moses. Thus, John's Gospel reflects an environment like that exemplified by Philo, in which Jewish versions of such ascent traditions existed.

9. Philo exemplifies the kind of Jewish milieu that serves as background for John's elaborations on the Jesus logion about God as sender and he himself as the one sent from heaven to earth. To Philo, Logos and angels serve as ambassadors from the heavenly God and king to the human beings on earth.

10. In John 6:31–58 Jesus identifies himself with the bread from heaven, which like the law of Moses came down to give life to the world. Philo combines wisdom, the Law, and manna in *On the Change of Names* §§253–63, where it is said that the manna raining down from heaven is the heavenly Sophia, Wisdom, which is in particular sent from above on the Sabbath, that is, when the laws of Moses are read and expounded.

11. When Philo saw Moses placed next to God and appointed god and given as a loan to the earthly region, then he had to face the problem of ditheism with regard to Moses, corresponding to what John faced in his Christology. In different ways both solved the problem

by emphasizing that Moses and Jesus, respectively, were entirely dependent on God.

Thus, instead of interpreting John against the background of Philo's Platonizing views as Dodd did, the present study demonstrates that other points from Philo exemplify the kind of Jewish traditions, thought categories, and historical contexts that were formative elements in John's background. Such traditions are at the same time interpreted along different lines by Philo and by John. Dodd's study suggests, however, some degree of kinship between some of the Jewish traditions and ideas and Platonizing and other ideas in the surrounding Greco-Roman world.

Notes

1. English translations of Philo's works are adapted from *Philo: With an English Translation* (ed. and trans. F. H. Colson and G. H. Whitaker; 10 vols.; Loeb Classical Library; Cambridge: Harvard University Press, 1929–62) and from *Philo: Supplement* (trans. R. Marcus; 2 vols.; Loeb Classical Library; Cambridge: Harvard University Press, 1953). Bible translations are my own.
2. C. H. Dodd, *The Interpretation of the Fourth Gospel* (Cambridge: Cambridge University Press, 1953), 133–43.
3. Ibid., 142.
4. Ibid., 142–43.
5. Ibid., 202–4.
6. Ibid., 56.
7. Ibid., 56–57.
8. See ibid., 58; Dodd's translation.
9. Ibid., 179–86.
10. Ibid., 66–67.
11. Ibid., 68.
12. Ibid.
13. Ibid., 274–75.
14. Ibid., 276.
15. Ibid., 277.
16. See R. E. Brown *The Gospel according to John* (Anchor Bible 29; Garden City: Doubleday, 1966), 1.522–23. Moreover, there are parallels with the ideas of Logos and Wisdom in gnostic writings, such as in the tractate *Trimorphic Protennoia*. C. Colpe and others

see Jewish wisdom traditions behind both *Trimorphic Protennoia* and John's prologue. Thus, the Old Testament and Jewish wisdom ideas were adapted along various lines, such as in Platonizing directions (Philo), gnostic mythological directions (*Trimorphic Protennoia*), and the Jesus traditions in John's Gospel. See C. Colpe, "Heidnische, jüdische und christliche Überlieferung in den Schriften aus Nag Hammadi III," *Jahrbuch für Antike und Christentum* 17 (1974): 109–25, esp. 122; K. Rudolph, *Gnosis* (Edinburgh: T. & T. Clark, 1983), 280–82; C. A. Evans, "On the Prologue of John and the Trimorphic Protennoia," *New Testament Studies* 27 (1981): 395–401; G. W. MacRae, "The Jewish Background of the Gnostic Sofia Myth," *Novum Testamentum* 12 (1970): 86–101.

17. E. Haenchen, "Probleme des johanneischen 'Prologs,'" *Zeitschrift für Theologie und Kirche* 60 (1963): 305n. 3. Cf. Psalms 33:6.

18. See P. Borgen, *"Logos Was the True Light" and Other Essays on the Gospel of John* (Trondheim: Tapir, 1983), 99–100; idem, *Philo, John, and Paul: New Perspectives on Judaism and Early Christianity* (Atlanta: Scholars Press, 1987), 76–78.

19. The term *he that sees* is an etymological interpretation of the name *Israel*, which was given to Jacob at Jabbok (Genesis 32:28). The term *the Name of God* may refer to Exodus 23:20–21, especially to the words about the angel, "my name is on him." Philo quotes this passage in *On the Migration of Abraham* §174 and identifies the angel with the divine Logos. In *3 Enoch (Hebrew Apocalypse)* 12.5 and Babylonian Talmud, tractate *Sanhedrin* 38b the angel of Exodus 23:20 is identified as Metatron. See P. Borgen, "Heavenly Ascent in Philo: An Examination of Selected Passages," in *The Pseudepigrapha and Early Biblical Interpretation* (ed. J. H. Charlesworth and C. A. Evans; Journal for the Study of the Pseudepigrapha Supplement 14/Studies in Scripture in Early Judaism and Christianity 2; Sheffield: JSOT Press, 1993), 258–59.

20. Borgen, *"Logos Was the True Light,"* 99–94; idem, *Philo, John, and Paul,* 84.

21. H. A. Wolfson, *Philo* (Cambridge: Cambridge University Press, 1948), 1.253–61.

22. For the following, see P. Borgen, "Creation, Logos and the Son: Observations on John 1:1–18 and 5:17–18," *Ex Auditu* 3 (1987): 89–92.

23. N. Walter, *Der Thoraausleger Aristobulus* (Berlin: Akademie Verlag, 1964), 170–71; P. Borgen, "Philo of Alexandria," in *Jewish Writings of the Second Temple Period: Apocrypha, Pseudepigrapha, Qumran Sectarian Writings, Philo, Josephus* (ed. M. E. Stone; Compendia rerum iudaicarum ad Novum Testamentum 2.2; Assen: Van Gorcum/ Philadelphia: Fortress, 1984), 277; idem, *"Paul Preaches Circumcision*

and Pleases Men" and *Other Essays on Christian Origins* (Trondheim: Tapir, 1983), 180, 184–85; and idem, *Philo, John, and Paul,* 12.

24. According to rabbinic exegesis, the Sabbath commandment does not forbid one to carry something about in one's house on the Sabbath. God's homestead is the upper and lower worlds. He may thus be active within it without coming into conflict with the Sabbath (*Genesis Rabbah* 30.6).

25. It is difficult to know with certainty exactly from where the quotation is taken. See P. Borgen, *Bread from Heaven: An Exegetical Study of the Concept of Manna in the Gospel of John and the Writings of Philo* (Novum Testamentum Supplement 10; Leiden: Brill, 1965), 40–42; R. Schnackenburg, *Das Johannesevangelium* (Herders theologischer Kommentar zum Neuen Testament; Freiburg: Herder, 1971), 2.54.

26. C. K. Barrett, *The Gospel according to St. John* (2d ed.; London: SPCK, 1978), 300.

27. In Philo's commentary entitled *Questions and Answers on Genesis,* a question or a specific view is introduced by simple formulas, for example by phrases such as "some say" (*Questions and Answers on Genesis* 1.8; 2.64; 3.13; cf. *On the Creation of the World* §77) or "why" (*Questions and Answers on Genesis* 1.1; 2.13, 64; etc.) or "what" (2.15, 59).

28. Borgen, *Bread from Heaven,* 80–83.

29. In Jesus' answer the phrase *he who believes* in John 6:47 refers back to 6:35 and 6:29–30, and the words *I am the bread of life* in 6:48 repeat 6:35, which in turn is the interpretation of the word *bread* in the scriptural quotation in 6:31.

30. Borgen, *Bread from Heaven,* 80–83.

31. Cf. also *Questions and Answers on Genesis* 2.28: *The question:* "What is the meaning of the words 'He brought the spirit over the earth and the water ceased'?" *Interpretation:* "Some would say that by 'spirit' is meant the wind through which the flood ceased." *Objection and alternative interpretation:* "But I myself do not know of water being diminished by wind.... Accordingly, (Scripture) now seems to speak of the spirit of the Deity."

32. Borgen, *Bread from Heaven,* 63–64, 61–67.

33. For example, in *The Worse Attacks the Better* §§47–48 Philo discusses two possible readings of the Greek translation of Genesis 4:8: "*Cain rose up against Abel his brother and slew him* (*auton*). It must be read in this way: *Cain rose up and slew himself* (*heauton*), not someone else."

34. In the exposition a. is paraphrased in §162b: "You see that the soul is fed ... with such words as God shall have poured like rain *out of ...* heaven." Line b. is paraphrased in §§163–67a; part of §163 reads: "To proceed, *The people ...* is to go out and make a beginning

of knowledge, not all at once but *the day's portion for a day.*" Line c. is paraphrased in §§167b–68. Part of §167b reads: "And this is why he goes on with the words *that I may prove them whether they will walk in My law or not.*"

35. See Borgen, *"Paul Preaches Circumcision and Pleases Men,"* 87–88; idem, *Philo, John, and Paul,* 65–68; idem, "Creation, Logos and the Son," 90–91; and idem, "The Sabbath Controversy in John 5:1–18 and Analogous Controversy Reflected in Philo's Writings," *Studia philonica* 3 [Earle Hilgert Festschrift] (1991): 209–21.

36. J. L. Martyn, *History and Theology in the Fourth Gospel* (2d ed.; Nashville: Abingdon, 1979), 70–71.

37. J. L. Martyn, "Source Criticism and Religionsgeschichte in the Fourth Gospel," in *The Interpretation of John* (ed. J. Ashton; Issues in Religion and Theology 9; Philadelphia: Fortress/London: SPCK, 1986), 113.

38. Cf. Barrett, *Gospel according to St. John,* 255.

39. Ibid., 206–7.

40. See P. Borgen, "God's Agent in the Fourth Gospel," in *Religions in Antiquity: Essays in Memory of Erwin Ramsdell Goodenough* (ed. J. Neusner; Studies in the History of Religions 14; Leiden: Brill, 1968), 137–48, esp. 146; repr. in Borgen, *"Logos Was the True Light,"* 121–32; in idem, *Philo, John, and Paul,* 171–84; and in *The Interpretation of John* (ed. J. Ashton; Issues in Religion and Theology 9; Philadelphia: Fortress/London: SPCK, 1986), 67–78.

41. John sees humans as a totality, while Philo has a dichotomic anthropology. Philo, however, keeps the Jewish understanding that both body and mind are created and that Moses' ascent included both, as can be seen in *On the Life of Moses* 2.69–70. See also Borgen, *Bread from Heaven,* 182; cf. 118–212. The question can be raised whether Philo's idea of second birth here depends on Hellenistic ideas of rebirth such as those found in Hermetic teachings. According to *Corpus Hermeticum* tractate 13 (entitled "Concerning Rebirth"), in rebirth the father is the will of god, the womb Wisdom, the seed the real good, and the offspring a god, a child of god; see Dodd, *Interpretation of the Fourth Gospel,* 44. One obvious difference between John and this Hermetic tractate should be mentioned: in the Hermetic teaching Wisdom serves as mother-womb, while both Philo and John assert that no mother is involved in the second birth.

42. E. Stein, "Der Begriff der Palingenesie im talmudischen Schrifttum," *Monatschrift für Geschichte und Wissenschaft des Judentums* 83, n.f. 47 (1939): 194–205; E. Sjäberg, "Wiedergeburt und Neuschöpfung im palästinischen Judentum," *Studia Theologica* 4 (1951): 44–85.

43. *Song of Songs Rabbah* 8.2 §1; adapted from *Midrash Rabbah* (trans. H. Freedman and M. Simon; London: Soncino, 1961), 9.303.

44. S. Buber (ed.), *Midrash Tanhuma* (Jerusalem: Ortsel, 1963–64).

45. The exegetical basis for this interpretation is the alternative derivation of the verbal form in Exodus 4:12 from the Hebrew verb meaning "conceive" (cf. 2:2).

46. Stein, "Der Begriff," 196–97.

47. This interpretation of birth from above shows that a Jesus logion was understood in a way that reflects that Judaism and Johannine Christianity were part of the Hellenistic thought world in which the ideas of rebirth were not uncommon. See Barrett, *Gospel according to St. John*, 206–7.

48. Philo can also interpret the Temple cosmologically: the heavenly Temple is the highest and truly holy Temple. He does not in this way ignore the earthly Temple made by hands, however, but the spiritual and the cosmic realities have constitutive significance; *On the Special Laws* 1.66–67.

49. Cf. Brown, *Gospel according to John*, 1.cxliv; and idem, " 'Other Sheep Not of This Fold': The Johannine Perspective on Christian Diversity in the Late First Century," *Journal of Biblical Literature* 97 (1978): 11.

50. Moreover, John's Gospel reflects a situation in which the Johannine community had moved into the broader world of other nations, as indicated by John's reference to Samaritans (John 4), Greeks (7:35; 12:20–21), and "other sheep not of this fold" (10:16).

51. See Borgen, "Heavenly Ascent in Philo," 263–67.

52. Qumran fragment 4Q491 11.1.12–19 also probably describes the ascent of a human being. See M. Smith, "Two Ascended to Heaven — Jesus and the Author of 4Q491," in *Jesus and the Dead Sea Scrolls* (ed. J. H. Charlesworth; New York: Doubleday, 1992), 290–301; C. A. Evans, "The Recently Published Dead Sea Scrolls and the Historical Jesus," in *Studying the Historical Jesus: Evaluations of the State of Current Research* (ed. B. Chilton and C. A. Evans; New Testament Tools and Studies 19; Leiden: Brill, 1994), 563–65.

53. H. Odeberg, *The Fourth Gospel* (Uppsala: Almqvist, 1929), 72–94; N. A. Dahl, "The Johannine Church and History," in *Current Issues in New Testament Interpretation* (ed. W. Klassen and G. F. Snyder; New York: Harper, 1962), 141; Borgen, *Bread from Heaven*, 185. The interpretation of John 3:13 is difficult; see P. Borgen, "Some Jewish Exegetical Traditions as Background for Son of Man Sayings in John's Gospel (Jn 3:13–14 and Context)," in *L'Évangile de Jean* (ed. M. de Jonge; Leuven: Leuven University Press, 1977), 243–45; and F. J. Moloney, *The Johannine Son of Man* (2d ed.; Rome: LAS, 1978), 54.

54. God, the King of kings, the Lord of all, comes down from the boundaries of heaven to God's house; i.e., the soul that is fitted to receive him (*On the Cherubim* §§99–100). God's potencies will descend from heaven with laws and ordinances to sanctify those who dwell on earth, provided that the soul-house of God is raised among them (§106).

55. Borgen, "God's Agent in the Fourth Gospel"; J.-A. Bühner, *Der Gesandte und sein Weg im 4. Evangelium* (Tübingen: Mohr [Siebeck], 1977). Cf. F. H. Agnew, "The Origin of the NT Apostle-Concept: A Review of Research," *Journal of Biblical Literature* 105 (1986): 75–96; M. M. Mitchell, "New Testament Envoys in the Context of Greco-Roman Diplomatic and Epistolary Conventions: The Example of Timothy and Titus," *Journal of Biblical Literature* 111 (1992): 641–62.

56. The Jesus logion found in John 13:20 ("he who receives any one whom I send receives me; and he who receives me receives him who sent me") has a firm place in the Gospel tradition, as seen from the parallels in Matthew 10:40; Mark 9:37; Luke 9:48; 10:16; and from the variations present in John 5:23; 8:19; 12:44–45; 14:7, 19; 15:23. See P. Borgen, "The Use of Tradition in John 12.44–50," *New Testament Studies* 26 (1979): 18–35; idem, "*Logos Was the True Light*," 49–66. In the Old Testament the principles of agency are present in an embryonic form, such as God's word when the people rejected Samuel: "They have not rejected you, but they have rejected me" (1 Samuel 8:7).

57. See *Tanhuma,* Shemoth 25 (ed. Buber); *Mekilta* on Exodus 15:26; *Exodus Rabbah* 29.9.

58. Manna is identified with the law in *Mekilta* on Exodus 13:17. See further Borgen, *Bread from Heaven,* 148–50.

59. See especially W. A. Meeks, *The Prophet-King: Moses Traditions and the Johannine Christology* (Novum Testamentum Supplement 14; Leiden: Brill, 1967), 103–5.

60. Moses is here seen as sharing in God's nature, so that at his death he is not "added" like others. He is translated (Deuteronomy 34:5) through that Word by which the whole cosmos was formed. In this way Moses is the prototype of the wise man (*On the Sacrifices of Abel and Cain* §§8, 10).

Chapter 4

John and the Synoptics: Historical Tradition and the Passion Narrative

D. Moody Smith

I

For a long time, indeed, since the end of the second century, Christians, and more recently modern critics, have assumed that John knew the other Gospels, the Synoptics, and wrote in cognizance of them, approving them.[1] Apparently John was later than the others in being accepted by the early Church as authoritative. When the Fourth Gospel was accepted, toward the end of the second century, most early Christian writers believed it had been written by John, the disciple of the Lord, with the other Gospels in view. The status of its author as an eyewitness and apostle presumably justified its obvious independence and differences from the Synoptics, which were already accepted as authoritative. Its many differences from the Synoptics were a potential problem. Less than a fourth of the Johannine narrative or other materials is found in the Synoptics, and vice versa. There are also some seeming contradictions. Apparently, some conservative second-century Christians did not accept John.[2] But some heretical Christians, later called gnostics and Montanists, liked it a lot. Gaius of Rome, an elder of the Roman church, is cited by Eusebius of Caesarea as an opponent of the Fourth Gospel, quite possibly because of the heterodox friends it had made. He was soon refuted by Bishop Hippolytus of Rome, who wrote *Defense of the Revelation and Gospel of John*. Heracleon, also of Rome, was a Valentinian gnostic who wrote the first commentary on John at mid-second century. When Irenaeus defended John's authority toward the end of the second century, he refuted gnostic interpretations of the prologue.

Origen, perhaps the early Church's greatest intellect, wrote his commentary on John in the first half of the third century. He pointed out the efforts of other interpreters to reconcile John with the Synoptics on the historical plane, but he rejected their efforts as fruitless (*Commentary on the Gospel of John* 10.2). Presumably he would have agreed with his mentor, Clement of Alexandria, who saw in John the spiritual Gospel, as distinct from the Synoptics, which recorded the bodily, or historical, facts (see Eusebius, *Ecclesiastical History* 6.14.7). So John became a part of the New Testament canon of scripture, fittingly as the Fourth Gospel, written in light of the others and therefore written last. Already Tatian had composed a harmony of the four Gospels, fitting the Synoptic material into the three-year framework of John. The Synoptics present a ministry of only one Passover, and presumably less than a year; John has three successive Passovers and thus a ministry of between two and three years.

Things did not change much until the modern, critical period. In the nineteenth century the authorship of the Fourth Gospel became a burning issue, as increasingly its attribution to John son of Zebedee was questioned. By the end of the twentieth century, scholars who affirm Johannine authorship had become a minority, although a great many had decided that agnosticism is the only appropriate attitude to the authorship question. At the beginning of the twentieth century, although confidence in Johannine authorship had faded, it was still assumed that John had known the Synoptics and wrote in light of them. But the end was not yet! In Germany Hans Windisch rejected the traditional belief that John wrote in order to supplement the Synoptics, to be supplemented by them, or to interpret them.[3] Rather, John uses so little of the other Gospels because he regards them as inadequate for expressing the essential meaning of the Christian message. Thus he omitted most of their content. In England, Cambridge scholar Percival Gardner-Smith questioned the assumption that John knew the Synoptics at all.[4] Why should we assume that he did? Is it not easier to explain the similarities without assuming dependence than to explain the great differences on the assumption that John was using Mark or any of the Synoptics? Gardner-Smith made a great impression on subsequent scholarship, and by the mid-to-late sixties a consensus had developed.[5] John is an independent Gospel. The author did not use the Synoptics in composing his Gospel, even if he knew of them, but relied on other sources or traditions. The situation is ambiguous, however, for John sometimes seems to presuppose knowledge we gain from the Synoptics; for example, that Jesus would be crucified and raised from the dead (John 2:21–22). There are at a few points substantial word-for-word agreements between John and the Synoptics, particularly Mark. For example, Jesus says to a sick man, "Arise, take up your pallet and walk [or go home]" (John 5:8; Mark 2:9).[6] For the most part, Markan materials found in John are in the same order as in Mark. Perhaps not surprisingly, it is once again widely believed that John knew and used at least Mark, if not all the Synoptics, but at what stage of composition and to what extent is much debated.[7]

In the background of this whole issue, and sometimes in the foreground, is the question of whether John is an independent source of knowledge of Jesus himself, that is, of the historical Jesus. C. H. Dodd, in his important book *Historical Tradition in the Fourth Gospel,* sought to demonstrate that John is independent of other Gospels and that the author used traditions of historical value.[8] The whole question of John and the Synoptics, and the related question of John's historical value, can be profitably considered by looking at the Passion Narratives. There John is closest to the Synoptics, but also manifests significant differences. In the rest of this essay, I wish to look at some significant cases in the Passion Narrative.

II

One cannot now consider any aspect of the Passion Narrative without paying attention to the massive, minute, and definitive analysis by R. E. Brown in *The Death of the Messiah.*[9] I should say in advance that I tend to agree with Brown because of his erudition, comprehensiveness, and balanced, critical judgment.

Brown believes that John's Passion Narrative is basically independent of the Synoptics.[10] Moreover, he thinks that Mark had before him a pre-Gospel or pre-Markan narrative as he wrote the story of Jesus' final hours.[11] Brown's reasoning in *The Death of the Messiah* about the independence of John is the same as in his Anchor Bible commentary. While much of John's distinctive material can easily be explained in the light of his theological interests, there are many differences, particularly in parallel narratives, that cannot be so explained. Let me give two examples that are, so to speak, on opposite sides of the fence. Pilate's question to Jesus about his kingship and Jesus' answer that his kingship is not of this world (John 18:36) can easily be understood as John's embroidery of Mark's narrative or of a common narrative. So that can be chalked up to John's distinctive theological interest. On the other hand, that Mark has Jesus crucified at the third hour, or 9:00 A.M. (Mark 15:25) — while in John he is still being tried before Pilate at the sixth hour, or noon (John 19:14) —

is hard to understand as a change John made for theological purposes.[12] We shall now look at several of these differences in the Johannine narrative that, on the assumption of John's use of Mark or the Synoptics, are hard to understand simply as deliberate or theologically motivated alterations of a Synoptic source or *Vorlage*. Moreover, if on substantial grounds John's different account seems more plausible historically, the Fourth Gospel's independence is corroborated. Either John is independent of the Synoptics or the evangelist believed he had superior information.

At the beginning of the passion story Mark notes that two days before Passover the chief priests and the scribes were seeking to arrest Jesus and put him out of the way (Mark 14:1-2). In Mark (and the Synoptics) Jesus has already entered Jerusalem three days before (11:1-10).[13] This Markan report of the plot against Jesus is followed immediately by the story of the anointing of Jesus by an unnamed woman during a supper given at the house of Simon the leper in Bethany (14:3-9). John has a similar story of the anointing of Jesus by a woman, Mary, the sister of Martha and Lazarus, at a supper in their house in Bethany (12:1-8). The stories are not identical, but it is hard to believe they represent two separate incidents. Matthew is here closely parallel to Mark, but Luke has no such story in this context. Instead, Luke has an anointing story set at a supper in Galilee (7:36-50), in the house of a Pharisee (7:36), whose name turns out to be Simon (7:40).

Strikingly, the anointing in John is also immediately preceded in that Gospel by an account of the Jewish authorities' plotting against Jesus (11:45-53). In John it is a meeting of the council (Sanhedrin) and obviously a more formal occasion (although not, strictly speaking, a trial) in which Caiaphas advises that Jesus be put out of the way lest the signs he performs lead to an intervention by the Roman authorities that would be disastrous for the Temple and the nation (11:48). It is remarkable that high priestly opposition is here portrayed as motivated by the possible response of the Romans to Jesus' activity. Since John portrays Jesus' public messiahship as a manifestation of signs, it is not too much to suggest that Caiaphas is really suggesting that Jesus' messianic activity is likely to provoke the Roman authorities.

In the Johannine trial before Pilate, however, the chief priests and Temple authorities actually have difficulty getting the Roman procurator to act against Jesus. "The Jews" are, of course, Jesus' chief antagonists, and Pilate comes across as his, admittedly ambivalent, defender. The point is that Caiaphas's portrayal of the likely attitude of the Romans seems to run counter to Pilate's attitude in the trial scene. Stranger things than this have happened. Yet it is worth observing that John 11:45–53 does stand in some tension with the trial before Pilate, even as it presents a plausible religious and political attitude on the part of the chief priests.

John supplies motivation for the chief priests' hostility to Jesus, which he could have added to the Markan account. But in this scene the motivation of Caiaphas is to forestall a Roman reaction, while in the trial scene the chief priests' goal is to motivate the Romans, that is Pilate, to act against Jesus! It is at least conceivable that John 11:45–53 indicates the chief priests' historical motives for wanting Jesus out of the way. He represents, or may arouse, a threat to the Temple and the nation, and the implicit threat to the high priestly authority and the concordat with the Romans is unspoken, but nevertheless clear. The portrayal of the role of Pilate in protecting Jesus may be a Johannine way of further condemning the Jews.

That the trial before Pilate represents the protocol of an actual dialogue is scarcely conceivable. Apparently John has elaborated the scene to bring out his theological interests and to underscore the guilt of the Jewish, particularly high priestly, authorities. Perhaps John used a simpler, briefer account, like Mark, if not Mark itself. Perhaps John's theological and related interests prevent his seeing the tension between the Roman attitude as suggested by Caiaphas and that manifested by Pilate. But while John's account of the Sanhedrin hearing is written in what is manifestly his distinct narrative style, it is not thereby proved to be without historical substance, and, as the very tension with the obviously Johannine narrative of the Pilate trial suggests, it may have some historical basis. It is difficult to imagine that John simply created the Caiaphas scene on the basis of Mark. A comparison of the Markan and Johannine anointing scenes raises similar, but more difficult, problems if Mark is taken to be the source of John.[14] These can be summarized by saying that the Markan account (14:3–9) is lucid, well rounded off, and presents no difficulties, while the Johannine (12:1–8) is none of these. In Mark the woman anoints Jesus' head (normal for a royal anointing); in John his feet. In John, Judas is named as the one who protests the act, which actually is what we might expect in John, who reports further that Judas kept the money box and stole from it (cf. 13:29). It is strange, however, that John, who denigrates Judas even more than do the other Gospels, reports that he was in effect the treasurer of the group. Apparently independently of the Synoptics who do not report this, John regards it as a historical fact. John gives Jesus' saying about the poor being always with you, but omits Mark's proviso that one can always do good for them. In Mark, Jesus says simply that the woman anointed Jesus' body beforehand for burial, which makes perfectly good sense. John would have changed that to read, "Let her keep it for the day of my burial." But she has already used it! Mark rounded off the story beautifully: "Wherever the gospel is preached in the whole world, what she has done will be told in memory of her."[15] John would have omitted that. We could perhaps understand the naming of the personae in John (12:1–8: Mary, Martha, and Lazarus) as Johannine embellishment of the Markan story, like the introduction of Judas. Otherwise, the Johannine changes, if that is what they are, represent the introduction of puzzling items into an otherwise clear account or the omission of matters in which John as well as Mark might have had an interest. Arguably, John had no interest in the woman memorialized in Mark, but then Mark does not name *her* and John does name *Mary,* the friend of Jesus who is the heroine of his story! John's account is hard to understand as derivative from Mark, but it is not clear that it presents fewer historical difficulties. That it is less carefully crafted may speak on the side of its traditional character, if not its historicity.

If one considers both Johannine stories as derivative from Mark, and they are juxtaposed in the same order in both, there are difficulties of one sort in one story and of another sort in the other in John. Mark then follows the anointing story with the preparation for the Passover (Mark 14:12–17), in which Jesus either demonstrates he has planned carefully or exhibits uncanny knowledge, probably the latter. If he were following Mark, John would have omitted that story, although it demonstrates the kind of knowledge and power typical of the Johannine Jesus. Instead, John would have placed the anointing directly before an account of the triumphal entry (John 12:12–19), which had taken place previously in Mark 11:1–10. A couple of comments related to the entry are in order.

First, as we have just observed, John omits Mark's story of the preparation for the entry, where Jesus also manifests uncanny knowledge. Then John has Jesus anointed on the eve of his entry into Jerusalem, and after he arrives there he does not retreat to Bethany. In Mark the anointing occurs on one of the several nights Jesus spent in Bethany during holy week. In fact, from Mark one gets the impression that Jesus stayed in Bethany every evening and walked a couple of miles into and back from Jerusalem every day. Mark's portrayal is quite plausible. It is not obvious that John's version is more likely historically. There were many pilgrims in Jerusalem at Passover, and probably not all could be accommodated in the city itself.

Yet Mark does use the Bethany motif to good literary and theological effect. Jesus curses the fig tree on the way into Jerusalem from Bethany (Mark 11:12–14). The next morning, after the cleansing of the Temple the previous day, the disciples see the tree withered as they head back to Jerusalem

(11:20). The fate of the fig tree seems to symbolize that of the Temple. Mark's narrative is replete with theological interests. Matthew abandons that framing, while Luke omits the cursing of the fig tree altogether (but cf. Luke 13:6–9). Given John's view of the relation of Jesus to the Temple, Mark's framing of the cleansing with Jesus' lodging in Bethany and cursing of the fig tree could have served John well, even though he placed the cleansing at the beginning of the ministry. In John's view Jesus displaced the Temple, which, if not accursed, has certainly withered (see the Johannine account of the Temple cleansing, esp. John 2:19–22).

So, in Mark Jesus enters Jerusalem, looks around the Temple (Mark 11:11), and retires to Bethany; then he returns to Jerusalem, on the way cursing the fig tree (11:12–14). He cleanses the Temple (11:15–17), and the next morning the disciples observe the fig tree withered (11:20) on the way back to Jerusalem (11:27). In John he simply stays in Jerusalem once he is there.

According to John, Jesus arrives in Bethany six days before Passover (John 12:1) and the next day (12:12) enters Jerusalem on Palm Sunday, the fifth day before Passover by John's reckoning. Counting backward from Mark's two days before Passover (Mark 14:1) — presumably Tuesday, since for Mark the Passover lamb would be slain on Thursday and the Feast of the Unleavened Bread would be held that evening — we arrive according to Mark's reckoning (cf. Mark 11:11, 12, 19, 20) at the triumphal entry on a Saturday, that is, Sabbath, the fifth day before Passover. This is unlikely historically.[16] On the other hand, if the feast is actually Friday evening, as it is according to John, the triumphal entry would be five days previous, or Sunday, as in *John's* reckoning. In the same Markan pericope (14:2), the chief priests decide to try to take Jesus captive *before* the feast, and that is what happens according to John's account, not Mark's. *That* plan to arrest Jesus, as well as the reckoning of the days forward and backward from that point in Mark, seem to favor the Johannine, rather than the Markan, chronology of the Passover.

In any event, it is clear that John's chronology of the passion week differs from the Synoptics in that, according to John, Jesus dies while the Passover lambs are being slain and before the Feast of the Unleavened Bread. In the Synoptics, of course, Jesus' last meal with the disciples, the Last Supper, is a Passover meal. The Johannine chronology reflects the identification of Jesus with the Passover lamb. "Christ, our paschal lamb, has been sacrificed," writes Paul (1 Corinthians 5:7). Of course, the paschal lamb is not, strictly speaking, a sin offering, and the evangelist makes little of cultic, sacrificial language in describing the effects of Jesus' death. (John 1:29 may be an exception to this; 1 John 2:2 clearly uses sacrificial terminology, but 1 John is probably the work of a different author.) The Gospel of John may reflect an alteration of the Passover chronology for theological effect, and, if so, this change may have already occurred at the pre-Gospel stage. (This coincides with 1 Corinthians 5:7 and accounts for the sacrificial elements of the Passover in the narrative that are not explicit in the theological discourses.) On the other hand, with Jesus in Jerusalem for Passover, and in view of the probability that Jesus' disciples celebrated his death at the immediately succeeding Passovers, it would have been natural for the earliest followers of Jesus to assume that the Last Supper was a Passover meal, even if it had not been so originally. (Perhaps not incidentally Paul refers to the Lord's supper as having been instituted by the Lord on the night when he was betrayed [1 Corinthians 11:23] with no reference to Passover; but in 5:7 he identifies Passover with his death.) For good reason Brown cautiously decides that the Johannine chronology of the passion week is historically correct.[17]

III

John differs from the Synoptics in the Passion Narrative in a few other points but may well be historically correct or more accurate. Most important is the absence of a formal trial before Jewish authorities in John. Jesus is taken before Annas, "the father-in-law of Caiaphas, who was high priest that year" (John 18:13). In John we read of no full-scale trial before the Sanhedrin: no formal witnesses and accusations, no verdict and condemnation. All these things are found in Mark (14:55–62), followed closely by Matthew. Luke strangely differs, as if he knew a conflicting account, such as we find in John: no nocturnal trial, only a morning assembly of the council from which the specifically juridical elements have been eliminated.[18]

Interestingly enough, in Mark's account of the trial Caiaphas is never named (Matthew identifies him); nor is Caiaphas named in Luke's account. Is John correct in naming Annas as the one before whom Jesus was taken and in not representing Jesus as having been formally tried? (Does Mark not name Caiaphas because the early tradition, which he knew, is silent about him?) If John used Mark, it is strange that he did not follow him in this respect, for the condemnation of Jesus by a formal trial before the highest Jewish council would have been a fitting culmination in the Fourth Gospel. Of course, John does say that Jesus was taken to the house of Caiaphas the high priest (John 18:24, 28; Mark 14:54; cf. Luke 22:54, which also indicates that Jesus was taken to the high priest's house); but he says nothing about what went on there. Is the reader supposed to supply the Markan/Matthean story? Alternatively, one may speculate that the visit to Caiaphas is a later editorial emendation inviting the reader to assume the Markan account at this point, and thus reconciling John with the Synoptics.[19]

John says that Jesus carried his own cross to Golgotha (John 19:17) and does not mention the role of Simon of Cyrene (Mark 15:21). Certainly John's description corresponds to the usual practice of the convicted man carrying the cross bar. Traditional Christian imagination usually portrays Jesus starting out bearing his own cross and needing help from Simon, obviously a harmonization of John and the Synoptics, but a quite plausible one.

Only John mentions the detail that the soldiers, at the behest of the Jews and the command of Pilate, were to break the legs of Jesus and those crucified with him in order to hasten their deaths (John 19:31), a common practice. (A similar account is found elsewhere only in the *Gospel of Peter*.) John, or the tradition, sees the fulfillment of scripture (Exodus 12:10, 46 and Psalms 34:20 in John 19:36; Zechariah 12:10 in John 19:37) in Jesus' legs not being broken, but rather his side pierced. Once again, what John alone reports is entirely plausible historically and has extrabiblical precedent. It is as reasonable to think that the earliest believers found scripture passages that conformed to events as it is to imagine that they always created events out of scripture passages.

As commentators frequently point out, the citation of Exodus 12:46 strongly suggests that Jesus fulfills the Passover. The inference that John must have adjusted his chronology accordingly is possible, but is not the only one suggested by historical logic. Possibly the death of Jesus as the lambs were being slain suggested the application of such a text in view of his legs not being broken. This would also explain why Jesus' death was interpreted as a sin offering *and* a Passover offering, despite the fact that the Passover lamb was not a sin offering. He "died for our sins" (1 Corinthians 15:3) while the Passover lambs were being slain.

Finally, John mentions neither the darkness at noon (Mark 15:33) and the rending of the veil of the Temple at Jesus' death (15:38 and parallels) nor the Roman centurion's confession (15:39 and parallels). I am not going so far as to maintain that John is silent because these were not actually historical events and that accordingly they found no place in the earliest tradition and the Johannine record! On the other hand, if John had Mark's account before him, it is hard to understand why he would have omitted these details. They fit so beautifully his Christology, particularly his view that Jesus' risen body displaced the Temple (John 2:21) and his presentation of the ministry of Jesus as the revelation of God's glory in this dark world, culminating at the long-waited hour of his death.

This survey at least shows that at many points in the Passion Narrative John differs from the Synoptics — in ways that both serve and do not serve his theological agenda. In cases where these differences do not serve his agenda, the possibility that they represent old tradition and possibly historical fact needs to be taken seriously. But even where they do serve John's theology or Christology, it is worth asking whether a traditional or historical item has for that reason been brought into play by John.

IV

We have, of course, made only a few probes into the Passion Narrative. Much more must be said and done. Yet the results are not insignificant. They justify the conclusion that where John differs from the Synoptics this Gospel needs to be taken seriously from a historical point of view. This point was made over a half century ago by Gardner-Smith and over thirty years ago by Dodd.

"John intended to write theology, not history," we say. Of no Gospel does such a statement seem a more apt characterization than of John. Yet no evangelist insists more strongly or directly on the importance of history and historical witness than John. Of course, John does not present history or biography in any modern sense of the terms. None of the evangelists do. Yet that the Johannine Jesus speaks the language of the heavenly Christ and of Christian theology should not cause us routinely to discount its historical value at all points. John may not intend to write history but theology, yet history is important for his theology.

What then about John's relation to the Synoptics? It is impossible to prove that John did not know the Synoptics. But, if he did, he chose to go his own way — doubtless because of his theological preoccupation and purpose, but also because he seems to possess (or know) alternative versions of accounts we know from the Synoptics. So while debate over John's relationship to other Gospels goes on, one thing is clear: John is, and intends to be, an independent Gospel.

Notes

1. For a summary of the situation in antiquity, see D. M. Smith, *John among the Gospels: The Relation in Twentieth-Century Research* (2d ed.; Columbia: University of South Carolina Press, 2001), 1–11.

2. For an exhaustive discussion of the evidence of opposition to John in antiquity, see J. D. Smith Jr., "Gaius and the Controversy over the Johannine Literature" (Ph.D. diss., Yale University, 1979).

3. H. Windisch, *Johannes und die Synoptiker: Wollte der vierte Evangelist die älteren Evangelien ergänzen oder ersetzen* (Untersuchungen zum Neuen Testament 12; Leipzig: Hinrichs, 1926).

4. P. Gardner-Smith, *Saint John and the Synoptic Gospels* (Cambridge: Cambridge University Press, 1938).

5. Smith, *John among the Gospels*, 45–84.

6. Bible translations are my own.

7. R. Bultmann is representative, although he was far from the first to see the influence of the Synoptics as falling on the later stages of its development or redaction. See his *The Gospel of John: A Commentary* (trans. G. R. Beasley-Murray; ed. R. W. N. Hoare and J. K. Riches; Philadelphia: Westminster, 1971); idem, *Das Evangelium des Johannes* (Göttingen: Vandenhoeck & Ruprecht, 1941). In this R. E. Brown agrees in principle in *The Gospel according to John* (2 vols.; Anchor Bible 29–29A; Garden City: Doubleday, 1966–70). More recently, however, a number of scholars, led by F. Neirynck of Louvain, argue that John's account is essentially based upon the Synoptics. See, for example, his valuable *Forschungsbericht:* "John and the Synoptics, 1975–1990," in *John and the Synoptics* (ed. A. Denaux; Bibliotheca ephemeridum theologicarum lovaniensium 101; Leuven: Leuven University Press, 1992), 3–62.

8. C. H. Dodd, *Historical Tradition in the Fourth Gospel* (Cambridge: Cambridge University Press, 1963).

9. R. E. Brown, *The Death of the Messiah: From Gethsemane to the Grave: A Commentary on the Passion Narratives in the Four Gospels* (2 vols.; New York: Doubleday, 1994).

10. Ibid., 75–93.

11. An appendix (ibid., 1492–1524) by M. L. Soards, one of Brown's former students, contains an impressive compendium of scholars who support a pre-Markan source.

12. Of course, if Mark is on Roman time and John on Jewish, they are not contradictory. Then Jesus would be crucified at the conclusion of the trial at noon, in John, and be crucified at three in the afternoon, in Mark. Yet John, if using Mark, leaves this contradiction still unexplained.

13. The reckoning of days in Mark prior to this (14:1–2) is somewhat uncertain, but it looks like we can discern the days. Clearly, 11:11 marks the end of the first day in Jerusalem, the day of the entry, as 11:12 speaks of the following (second) day. In 11:19 Jesus goes out of the city, presumably to Bethany for the evening, and on the morning of the next day, the third, the fig tree is seen withered (11:20). This day presumably continues as they enter Jerusalem (11:27) and Jesus engages in controversy in the Temple (11:27–12:40). Then he observes the poor widow making her contribution to the Temple treasury (12:41–44), after which he and his disciples leave the Temple for the Mount of Olives opposite it (13:3), where Jesus gives his so-called apocalyptic discourse.

14. See J. F. Coakley, "The Anointing at Bethany and the Priority of John," *Journal of Biblical Literature* 107 (1988): 241–56.

15. Cf. E. Schüssler Fiorenza, *In Memory of Her: A Feminist Theological Reconstruction of Christian Origins* (New York: Crossroad, 1986), xiii.

16. Of course, it is conceivable that Mark reckons Friday as the first day of Passover, in which case two days before would presumably be Wednesday and the triumphal entry would take place the first day of the week, on Sunday. There is, obviously, no reference to Sunday per se in the New Testament. "The first day of the week" does not occur in connection with the triumphal entry, only the resurrection. Palm Sunday is an inference from the Gospel accounts.

17. See Brown, *Death of the Messiah*, 1356–73, esp. 1372–73; but otherwise E. P. Sanders, *The Historical Figure of Jesus* (London: Penguin, 1993), 282–90, esp. 283–86.

18. On the possible influence of John on Luke, see M. A. Matson, *In Dialogue with Another Gospel? The Influence of the Fourth Gospel on the Passion Narrative of the Gospel of Luke* (Atlanta: Society of Biblical Literature, 2001).

19. Similarly John 2:12; 3:24; and 6:59 provide contacts with the Synoptic narrative and do not advance the Johannine narrative.

Chapter 5

Lady Wisdom and
Johannine Christology

James H. Charlesworth

Before the composition of the Fourth Gospel
and for over one thousand years, Israelites and Jews had
concentrated their genius on how the ineffable Creator communicates with his creation. One of the most impressive
insights obtained, through speculation and revelation, was
the concept of wisdom. This concept developed from the
wisdom *of* God to the Wisdom *from* God; that is to say,
the concept moved from a way of talking about God's attributes to a being, personified or hypostatic, that is separate
from God.

The beginning of such thought can be found in the
Psalms, Proverbs, Job, and Ecclesiastes. The thought devel-
oped consecutively through the so-called apocryphal books
to the early rabbinic writings. It appears significantly in
the Old Testament Apocrypha, especially in Sirach and the
Wisdom of Solomon. It is developed in the Old Testament
Pseudepigrapha, especially in documents such as *1 Enoch
(Ethiopic Apocalypse)*, Pseudo-Phocylides, *4 Maccabees*, the *Odes*

of Solomon, Syriac Menander, and the *Hellenistic Synagogal Prayers.* It is not dominant in the Dead Sea Scrolls, but does appear in some documents, notably *Dame Folly and Lady Wisdom* (4Q184) and *Beatitudes* (4Q525).[1] In the early rabbinic period it is found especially in the *Sayings of the Fathers.*

Scholars over the past two hundred years have labored to define wisdom.[2] Perhaps it is best to follow a definition found in antiquity, in *4 Maccabees.* In this pseudepigraphon, written sometime before 70 C.E. perhaps in Alexandria, we find in 1:16–17 the following: "Wisdom, I submit, is knowledge of things divine and human, and of their causes. And this wisdom, I assume, is the culture we acquire from the Law, through which we learn the things of God reverently and the things of men to our worldly advantage."[3] This definition of wisdom by an ancient Jew is helpful. Wisdom is what a wise and mature person would do in this world and in a culture defined by Torah, God's will. Thinking about Proverbs, L. G. Perdue rightly states that instruction in wisdom includes "knowledge about God, the world, and human life; the embodiment of sapiential piety and virtue; and the construction of a world for human dwelling."[4]

Recent wisdom research convinces me of the following:

1. No synthesis on wisdom is possible. In fact, it is unwise to omit or ignore outstanding aspects of wisdom that would be eliminated by any synthesis. Wisdom is defined by life experiences; and life extends beyond the borders of any abstract synthesis.
2. The most frequent genres within Wisdom literature are (a) the saying (appears in the indicative mood and is based on experience) and (b) the admonition (based on experience that appears in a positive and negative form).
3. Wisdom is not revelatory literature like prophetic pronouncements. It is literature based on practical experience and usually has nothing to do with the norms, traditions, or claims associated with the unique theology or concepts associated with Israel or Judaism.[5] While

the Hebrew term for wisdom, *khokmah,* probably originally meant only outstanding skill (e.g., in Job 5:13), it
obtained religious and ethical meanings by the Second
Temple period.[6]

4. Wisdom develops within Judaism until it is clearly
   personified as Lady Wisdom, especially in Sirach 24,
   Baruch 3–4, and Wisdom of Solomon 7–9. As such she
   is identified with Torah. I am convinced that early Jews,
   beginning in the second century B.C.E., were not satisfied
   only with the concept of personification, since they often
   portrayed Wisdom, like the highest of the archangels,
   as acting like a being separate from God; that is, she
   was a hypostatic being.[7] This insight may not be clear,
   since experts wisely wish to divorce the concept of a
   hypostatic Wisdom from the discussions regarding hypostasis during the christological debates of the fourth
   and fifth centuries C.E.

5. Wisdom does not command but persuades, especially
   in Proverbs. She brings into human society the divine
   voice. Wisdom is sometimes depicted as the one who is
   sent by God to humans. The best example of this concept
   is found in Sirach 24:

> Wisdom will praise herself,
>   and will glory in the midst of her people.
> In the assembly of the Most High she will open her
>   mouth,
>   and in the presence of his host she will glory:[8]
> "I came forth from the mouth of the Most High,
>   and covered the earth like a mist.
> I dwelt in high places,
>   and my throne was in a pillar of cloud.
> Alone I have made the circuit of the vault of heaven
>   and have walked in the depths of the abyss.
> In the waves of the sea, in the whole earth,
>   and in every people and nation I have gotten a
>   possession.
> Among all these I sought a resting place;
>   I sought in whose territory I might lodge.

> Then the Creator of all things gave me a commandment,
> and the one who created me assigned a place for my
> tent.
> And he said, 'Make your dwelling in Jacob,
> and in Israel receive your inheritance.'
> From eternity, in the beginning, he created me,
> and for eternity I shall not cease to exist.
> In the holy tabernacle I ministered before him,
> and so I was established in Zion."
>
> — Sirach 24:1–10 (RSV)[9]

6. Wisdom existed before creation and was with God and
   is therefore in some ways involved in the act of creating before time. This concept is evident in the preceding
   quotation.

Having briefly reviewed the broad consensus regarding the concept of wisdom in early Judaism, let me turn
to Johannine Christology. The major commentators make
clear that the Fourth Gospel is heavily edited and represents
two editorial stages with a much later insertion of the pericope about the adulteress (John 7:53–8:11). The additions to
the Fourth Gospel indicate, at least to me, that the developments in Christology grew from a belief in Jesus as the
promised Messiah to what it means cosmologically, ontolog-
ically, protologically, eschatologically, and sociologically to
believe in Jesus as Messiah; that is to say, the crises in the
Johannine community, especially the expulsion of believing
Jews from the synagogue, were not only sociological but also
cosmological. The believing Jews in the Johannine community were led to reflect on the meaning of the Christ, the
arrival of the one promised long ago by Isaiah, Jeremiah,
Zechariah, and especially Micah. Those reflections shifted
the interest in the end time (eschatology) by Jesus' earliest
followers to a penetrating breakthrough into the meaning of
the beginnings of time and space. These protological reflections led to the perception that the Christ (the Logos), like
Wisdom, existed before the creation of life and earthly and
interstellar space.

Johannine Christology also developed from a so-called
low Christology to a high Christology.[10] There is obviously
a significant development within the Johannine community.
This development is mirrored in the successive additions
to the Fourth Gospel. But, I must stress, the progression
of insight was by no means linear or a trajectory; it was
more like the forward flow of the Mississippi with successive
meanderings in virtually all directions.

It is relatively certain that the Fourth Gospel took shape
over decades, from the late 30s to the late 90s. It represents
the advanced symbolical thought of Jews living together with
Gentiles in a community that is obviously devoted to study
of and reflection on Torah and the relation between Jesus and
God. One of the final additions to the Fourth Gospel was most
likely the Logos hymn that now begins that Gospel. As the
Jews and Gentiles in the Johannine community — probably
a school — studied Torah and sought to understand Jesus'
place in salvation history, the dependence on Wisdom probably increased over time and hit its zenith, as we shall see,
in the Logos hymn. In the following study our focus will
be on the personification, indeed the hypostatization of wisdom as Lady Wisdom. We should not think that Wisdom
has supplied the framework or provided the model for the
Fourth Evangelist's Christology. Rather, we should imagine
that Wisdom has provided many of the paradigms on which
Johannine Christology developed.

Wisdom in Judaism

In Second Temple Judaism — that is, early Judaism — two ir-
reconcilable positions were expressed regarding the abode of
Wisdom. The apocalypses incorporated the idea that Wisdom
could not find a home on earth. This claim is related to the
apocalyptic theme that meaning and values can no longer
be found on earth. They can be obtained only from above,

in heaven, or from the future, from the future age. The *locus classicus* for this idea is found in 1 (*Ethiopic Apocalypse*) *Enoch* 42:

> Wisdom could not find a place in which she could dwell;
> but a place was found (for her) in the heavens.
> Then Wisdom went out to dwell with the children of the
>   people,
> but she found no dwelling place.
> (So) Wisdom returned to her place
> and she settled permanently among the angels.
> Then Iniquity went out of her rooms,
> and found whom she did not expect.
> And she dwelt with them,
> like rain in a desert,
> like dew on a thirsty land.[11]

This concept of Wisdom is not missing in the Fourth Gospel.[12] In this Gospel Jesus is portrayed as one who could not find a "home": "The world did not know him. He came to his own home, and his own people did not receive him" (John 1:10–11, my translation).

Like Wisdom, Jesus alone is from above; all others are from below. The Fourth Evangelist uses the technical terms *above* and *below* to explain his cosmologically salvific Christology. For example, he puts into the mouth of Jesus the following words: "You are from below (*ek tōn katō*), I am from above (*ek tōn anō*)" (John 8:23). The asyndetic contiguity between the two phrases — that is, the lack of any connecting particle like "but" — explains in penetrating depth the close connection between the two spheres, the *anō* and the *katō*. This is due to the pervasive influence of an ingenious incarnational Christology that is unique to the Fourth Evangelist: Jesus — Logos and Wisdom — was incarnate in the here and now of human suffering and anguish. So, unlike the Synoptics (Matthew, Mark, and Luke), Jesus stumbles to Golgotha carrying his own cross. Subsequently, after his excruciating death his corpse is stabbed unmercifully by a pagan. Rather than be naively docetic, the final edition of the Fourth Gospel has passages like these that prove how utterly human and vulnerable was the man Jesus. In fact, only in the Fourth Gospel are we told his name: Jesus son of Joseph (6:42).

Thus, the Fourth Evangelist's Christology contrasts somewhat with the apocalyptic notion that Wisdom could not find a home on earth (*1 Enoch* 42). In line with some apocryphal and pseudepigraphical books and early rabbinic literature, the Fourth Evangelist suggests that Wisdom in Jesus did find a place on earth. She briefly found a home in Israel. The earliest example of the concept that Wisdom found "a nesting place" in Israel seems to be Sirach 24:

> From eternity, in the beginning, he created me,
>   and for eternity I shall not cease to exist.
> In the holy tabernacle I ministered before him,
>   and so I was established in Zion.
> In the beloved city likewise he gave me a resting place,
>   and in Jerusalem was my dominion.
> I took root in an honored people,
>   in the portion of the Lord, who is their inheritance.
>   — Sirach 24:9–12 (RSV)

A similar thought is found in Baruch 3:36–37, which celebrates Wisdom:

> He (God) found the whole way to knowledge,
>   and gave her to his servant Jacob
>   and to Israel, whom he loved.
> Afterward she (Wisdom) appeared on earth
>   and lived with humankind.

According to the Qumran text entitled *Beatitudes* (4Q525), Wisdom is associated with Torah, which is the major emphasis developed in rabbinic tradition. Here is an excerpt from fragment 2, lines 3b–4a:

> Blessed is the man (Adam) who overtakes Wisdom,
> and walks continuously in the Torah of the Most High,
> and prepares his heart for her ways.[13]

The identification of Torah with Wisdom is also found in early rabbinic texts, especially in the *Sayings of the Fathers* 2.8:

"The more Torah, the more life; the more study, the more wisdom."[14] When working with ancient Hebrew or Greek it is not clear when to use capitals; this passage also could have been translated "the more Wisdom." What is the function of Wisdom in Jewish literature prior to and contemporaneous with the Fourth Gospel? She is portrayed as one calling, exhorting, and guiding those who seek her. She guides them to the way above. This exhortatory role of Wisdom is found in Wisdom literature from Proverbs 8 through Sirach 24 to the *Odes of Solomon* 33:

> Does not wisdom call,
> and does not understanding raise her voice?
> . . . .
> . . . she cries out:
> "To you, O people, I call,
> and my cry is to all that live."
> — Proverbs 8:1–4

> Come to me, you who desire me,[15]
> and eat your fill of my fruits.
> . . . .
> Whoever obeys me will not be put to shame,
> and those who work with my help will not sin.
> — Sirach 24:19, 22

> However the perfect Virgin stood,[16]
> who was preaching and summoning and saying:
> "O you sons of men, return,
> and you their daughters, come.
> And abandon the ways of that Corruptor,
> and approach me.
> And I will enter into you,
> and bring you forth from destruction,
> and make you wise in the ways of truth."
> — *Odes of Solomon* 33.5–8[17]

In *1 Enoch* 37–71 wisdom is an attribute of Enoch, who is identified as both the Son of Man and the Messiah. Enoch is given "the vision of wisdom" (37.1) and propounds "the words of wisdom" (37.2). He explains that Wisdom could not find an abode on earth and so returned to the heavens (42.1–3). As "that Son of Man," he is given a name before the creation of the world (48.2–3). Having become "the Chosen One," Enoch, as that Son of Man, reveals "the wisdom of the Lord of the Spirits to the righteous and the holy ones" (48.7). Being only obliquely identified as the Messiah (48.10),[18] Enoch is one before whom "wisdom flows like water" (49.1). In him, the Elect One, "dwells the spirit of wisdom" (49.3). These observations remove any doubt that the *Apocalypse of Enoch* is heavily indebted to wisdom traditions and literature.

While G. von Rad's claim that apocalyptic thought comes from Wisdom literature is too simplistic,[19] it is now clear that the sages who produced the apocalypses were deeply influenced by many strands of traditions and from many cultures. It is obvious that one of these traditions was wisdom. R. A. Coughenour argues rather persuasively that the passages that connect the various books of Enoch now incorporated into the *Apocalypse of Enoch* are imprinted with an emphasis on wisdom. That is, the final editor of these books, the one who brought them together into a library of Enoch books, had a purpose. In Coughenour's words, "the key to the compilation is the wisdom stance" of this final editor.[20] Henceforth, from this and many other studies on the relation of wisdom to apocalypsology,[21] we must not err and think with Kierkegaard of an "either-or" but of a "both-and." That is, the apocalypses show not only apocalypsology but also the pervasive and enduring importance of wisdom.

The conclusion is exceedingly important for a better understanding of Johannine Christology. It was influenced by many traditions within Judaism. It shows the both-and of early Jewish theology. One of the most powerful influences on it, as we shall see, is wisdom. Let us now shift our focus from an examination of wisdom traditions and ask how these ideas affected the expression and development of the Christology in the Fourth Gospel.

Wisdom in John's Christology

Far too often experts on the Fourth Gospel seek to show that the author was not influenced by apocalypticism. I am convinced that the author inherited much from apocalypticism but that it was not the main influence on him. Only two examples must suffice for the present. First, the evangelist alludes to Jewish apocalyptic thought when he has Jesus promise to Nathanael, and thus to others like him who believe, that he (Nathanael) will have a vision. He will see *heaven open* and the angels of God ascending and descending on the Son of Man (John 1:51). Second, the Fourth Evangelist creates a polemic against Jewish apocalypticism when he claims that no one — not even wise men like Enoch — had ascended into heaven. In fact, he attributes to Jesus the following contention: "No one has ascended into heaven except the one who descended from heaven, the Son of Man" (3:13). The concept of "the Son of Man" derives from Jewish apocalypticism.

Wisdom also significantly influenced the composition of the Fourth Gospel. Moreover, wisdom as a part of Jewish apocalypticism helped shape Johannine Christology.

We know that the Fourth Gospel has more than one editorial layer. The present form of the Gospel of John is really a second edition of this Gospel. Most likely John 21, 15–17, and 1:1–18 (among other passages) were added to an earlier, first edition. The christological development in the Johannine school seems to move from otherworldliness (apocalyptic wisdom) to the incarnation of divine and human. In a certain sense, the movement is from apocalypticism to rabbinicism. In this sense the Fourth Gospel is like *2 Baruch*, a Jewish apocalypse composed about the same time as the Fourth Gospel.

Among the many features of wisdom not found in the Fourth Gospel are the use of wisdom for royal rule and the acquisition of encyclopedic knowledge concerning plants, trees, and animals. Johannine Christology is quite unlike Job 28 and Baruch 3–4, according to which only God knows the

place of Wisdom. For the Fourth Evangelist, Wisdom is em-
bodied in Jesus, the Logos, and the Johannine community
puts its stamp on the incarnation of Wisdom by stressing
that "we have seen his glory, glory as of the only Son from
the Father" (John 1:14, my translation).

Perhaps influencing this stress on "the glory" of Jesus
is the concept of Wisdom who "will glory" not only "in the
midst of her people" but also "in the assembly of the Most
High" (Sirach 24:1–2). Another text found among the Dead
Sea Scrolls but not a Qumran sectarian composition, Psalm
154, is also important for understanding the pre-Johannine
Jewish emphasis on Wisdom's glory. Note the following
passage:

> For to announce the glory of the Lord,
> Wisdom has been given.
> And to recount his many deeds,
> She was made known to humanity.
> . . . .
> And a person who glorifies the Most High,
> He accepts as one who brings a meal offering,
> As one who offers he-goats and baby bulls;
> As one who anoints the altar with many burnt offerings;
> As sweet-smelling fragrance from the hand of the
>   righteous ones.
> — Psalms 154.5–11 (my translation)

As A. S. van der Woude points out, the purpose of Wisdom is
to glorify God, and this task "equals cultic sacrifices."[22] This
idea in Judaism would have been appealing to the Fourth
Evangelist, who stands out among the evangelists in stressing
the glory of Jesus.

As is patently obvious, Wisdom is portrayed in the biblical and parabiblical literature as a lady. Perhaps this concept
may be traced back to Proverbs 8–9, which may date from
so late as 200 B.C.E. In these verses some Jews would have
seen Wisdom as a refined lady. We have among the Qumran
Scrolls a document that is now called *Dame Folly and Lady
Wisdom* (4Q184). Dame Folly tries to lure men and take away
their wisdom.

What does this concentration on Lady Wisdom have to do with the Fourth Gospel, since the one who brings God's will to humans is a man, Jesus son of Joseph (John 6:42)? It is apparent that the Johannine Jews see in Jesus' life the presence of Wisdom. They thus shifted the concept from a female to a male. That is, in the Gospel, from 1:19 to the end, Logos is never mentioned. The Gospel is the portrait of a Jewish male. That is the main reason that Sophia appears in the prologue (1:1–18) as the Logos, which is masculine singular in grammatical form but not necessarily in thought. This is not the only reason why the Fourth Evangelist chose to use Logos over Sophia. Philo informs us of another aspect of Sophia. Philo contends that Sophia, the daughter of God, is a masculine concept for humans, because Sophia "engenders in souls a desire to learn discipline, knowledge... noble actions."[23] It is for both these reasons that the Fourth Evangelist probably chose Logos over Sophia.

In the first edition of the Fourth Gospel, Moses Christology is already apparent, as M.-É. Boismard and U. C. von Wahlde demonstrate. The feeding of the multitude at Passover time in 6:1–14 portrays Jesus as Moses. The point is particularly clarified in 6:14: "This is indeed the prophet who is to come into the world." The reference to "the prophet" is an intertextual echo of Deuteronomy 18:18, which contains God's promise to send a prophet like Moses. The link between the story of Jesus and the traditions related to Moses is made explicit in the same chapter. The author of the Fourth Gospel adds in 6:31–32 that the manna given in the wilderness was not supplied by Moses but was a gift from God (cf. 6:49). Jesus is now portrayed as the bread from heaven given by God.

This Moses-messianic expectation took on eschatological significance within postexilic Jewish theology and particularly within Samaritanism. The Samaritans expected at the end of the present eon the coming of the Taheb, the messianic prophet like Moses.[24] An echo of Moses-messianism may also be found in John 7:40, according to which some people claimed, "This is really the prophet." These reflections do not take us from our search for wisdom concepts, because the Samaritans believed that God created the angels through Wisdom.[25]

Also significant are the many metaphors the Fourth Evangelist apparently derived from Wisdom literature. According to Proverbs 3:18, Wisdom is "a tree of life to those who lay hold of her," which reminds us of the metaphor of the vine and branches, whereby only the one who remains attached to the vine, Jesus, has access to the vinedresser, the Father God (John 15:1). John 15 is reminiscent of the portrayal of Wisdom as the vine, according to Sirach 24:17:

> Like the vine I caused loveliness to bud,
>   and my blossoms became glorious and abundant fruit.

It is possible that the author of the Fourth Gospel has this text memorized, for he portrays Jesus as saying, "I am the true vine" (John 15:1). Jesus, like Wisdom, exhorts his followers, the branches, to abide in him so as to "bear much fruit" (15:8). In Sirach 24 and John 15 we find two beings sent by God — Wisdom and Jesus — who exhort those who love them to be linked to them, the vine. In Sirach 24:17 wisdom states, "I am like the vine"; this is very close to John 15:1, in which Jesus states, "I am the true vine." Making the connection between John and Sirach virtually undeniable is the idea of Wisdom's "blossoms" (those who are attached to her) becoming "glorious and abundant fruit." Those who remain with Jesus, the vine, will have "much fruit" (John 15:8).[26]

It is by looking to Wisdom literature that we can begin to understand a *prima facie* vulgar and unattractive concept in the Fourth Gospel — the eating of Jesus' flesh and the drinking of his blood. This image seems far removed from the attractive symbolism found in Paul and the Synoptics when they describe the Eucharist. Even further removed from the elevated metaphorical symbolism that characterizes the Fourth Gospel are these words: "Truly, truly, I say to you, unless you eat the flesh of the Son of Man and drink his blood, you do not have life in yourselves; he who gnaws my flesh and drinks my blood has eternal life" (John 6:53–54, my translation). It is shocking to read "gnaws" rather than the usual "eats," but the Greek verb used by the Fourth Evangelist is *trōgō*, and it means "to gnaw, nibble, munch." It is obvious why we should be astounded by a pagan concept in this highly advanced book of symbolisms. The answer cannot be obtained by looking to Greek thought, in which the verb indicates symbolically close friendship (e.g., the concept is of nibbling bread together [Polybius]). The problem may be resolved by looking at Wisdom literature. I do not want to suggest that all the problems can be resolved by examining the extensive links between the Fourth Gospel and Wisdom literature, but the following parallels help me comprehend this apparently revolting thought in the Fourth Gospel. According to Proverbs 9:5, Wisdom calls,

> Come, eat of my bread
> and drink of the wine I have mixed.

And according to Sirach 24:19–21 Wisdom explains,

> Come to me, you who desire me,
> and eat your fill of my fruits.
> For the memory of me is sweeter than honey,
> and the possession of me sweeter than the honeycomb.
> Those who eat of me will hunger for more,
> and those who drink of me will thirst for more.

It is as if the Fourth Evangelist inherits such thoughts and advances them when he applies them to Jesus. The one who eats the bread from heaven, Jesus or God's Wisdom, "will live forever" (John 6:58). And, as Jesus informs the anonymous Samaritan woman, the one who drinks the water he alone can supply will never thirst again (4:14). The full meaning of such passages becomes clearer when we see how wisdom traditions are reflected in them.

Let me now try to clarify how Lady Wisdom helped shape the presentation of Jesus Christ in the Fourth Gospel. I shall begin by looking at the first edition, which begins at John 1:19, although some portions of it may be found in earlier verses now incorporated in the prologue.

Wisdom and Jesus Symbolize Light and Mirror

Wisdom is portrayed as embodying light and is described as a mirror:

> For she (Wisdom) is a reflection of eternal light,
> a spotless mirror of the working of God,
> and an image of his goodness.
> — Wisdom of Solomon 7:26

A strikingly similar thought is attributed to the first Jewish theologian, Aristobulus, who uttered the following words: "And the same thing might be said metaphorically about Wisdom also. For all light has its origin in it. And some of those belonging to the Peripatetic school have said that Wisdom holds the place of a lantern; for as long as they follow it unremittingly, they will be calm through their whole life"[27] (5.9–10). These images and thoughts, especially light (*phōs*), are impressively similar to the portrayal of Jesus in the Fourth Gospel. Like Wisdom, Jesus is proclaimed to be the light of the world. In fact, these exact words are put on the lips of Jesus: "I am the light (*phōs*) of the world" (John 8:12). Such reflections demonstrate the broad base for wisdom traditions now reflected in the Fourth Gospel; this broad spectrum of wisdom traditions is missed in the secondary literature.

While the word *mirror* does not appear in the Fourth Gospel, the concept may be present when Jesus is reputed to have said, "And whoever sees me sees him who sent me" (John 12:45). The portrayal of Wisdom as a mirror (*esoptron*) evokes images associated with the Johannine school.[28] This idea explodes in memorable fashion in the *Odes of Solomon:*

Behold, the Lord is our mirror.
Open (your) eyes and see them in him.
— Odes of Solomon 13.1

Wisdom and Jesus Are Sent by God

Lady Wisdom has shaped the Johannine portrayal of the relation between Jesus and God in the phrase *he who has sent him* into the world. In Wisdom literature Lady Wisdom is sent by God into the world (Proverbs 8:30–31), and in the Fourth Gospel Jesus is sent into the world. They are both sent to humans by God. According to the Wisdom of Solomon, Wisdom is sent from the heavenly throne room (9:10); she is the "pure emanation of the glory of the Almighty" (7:25). The "sending" paradigm, expressed through the verbs *pempō* and *apostellō*,[29] is developed beautifully and completely in the Fourth Gospel in the farewell discourses, especially John 17. Jesus refers to his Father as "he (or him) who sent me." The disciples are those of whom Jesus may state, "I have sent them into the world" (17:18). One might think then that Jesus is categorized as "he who was sent," but this is inaccurate. John the Baptist is the one sent by God (1:6). Jesus, in contrast, is not the one sent into the world; he is no envoy.[30] Perhaps the Fourth Evangelist is avoiding a too neat synonym that would make Jesus simply Wisdom. The point seems crucial. According to the Fourth Evangelist, when one looks at Jesus he or she does not see one sent from God but rather "the Father who sent him" (5:23). Thus, for the Fourth Evangelist anyone who has seen Jesus "sees him who sent me" (12:45). This is a development beyond the wisdom tradition, because Jews did not believe that seeing Wisdom was tantamount to seeing God. That is to say, for the Fourth Evangelist Jesus is not like Wisdom, who is never equated with God. On the other hand, Jesus and God are one (17:22).

The concept of "one sent" is very old and deeply ingrained in Israelite and Jewish theology; it is found in many strata of thought from the Bible to the Mishnah (cf. Mishnah, tractate *Berakhot* 5.5). It is possible that there is little direct influence from wisdom here on the Fourth Gospel. But, it may be the combination of various themes that is decisive in revealing such a link. The paradigm of sending is linked with the concept of the above (*anō*) and below (*katō*). The evangelist stresses that Jesus is the only one from above and that those who believe in him must be born *anōthen*[31] (i.e., not only "again" but also "from above"). It is obvious that the link with the concept of Wisdom as one sent by God from above is surely in the mind of the evangelist when he writes his Gospel. Thus, the concept of Jesus and God expressed in the phrase *he who sent me into the world from above* is most likely shaped within the crucible inherited from wisdom in the Fourth Gospel.

According to Sirach 24:7–10 Lady Wisdom finds a home in Jerusalem. Has that concept influenced the Fourth Evangelist who, in sharp contrast to the Synoptics, centered Jesus' ministry not in Samaria or Galilee but in Jerusalem, where he spends approximately the last six months of his life? It will never be possible to define the borders of the influence of wisdom traditions on the Fourth Evangelist.

At this point another major difference between Wisdom and Jesus must be clarified. Both Wisdom and Jesus can be said to be in the world, but Jesus is not merely a personification. He, unlike Wisdom, is incarnate. In the Fourth Gospel — and only there — is he portrayed as exhausted, thirsty, and crying. Wisdom cannot obtain such human frailties.

A third major difference between Wisdom and Logos exists. Wisdom is created, but Logos was from the beginning. H. Ridderbos stresses this difference, pointing out that, in contrast to Logos or Word, Wisdom belongs "to the created world." He interprets John 1:1 as intending "to accentuate the line of demarcation that separates the Logos from that which has been created."[32] I am not certain that the intention of the author of 1:1 was to emphasize such a distinction between Logos and Wisdom; but some difference is evident.

Wisdom and Jesus Exhort

Lady Wisdom has influenced the portrayal of Jesus in the Fourth Gospel since, like Wisdom, Jesus calls and exhorts Israel (Proverbs 9:3; Sirach 24:19). As von Rad states, "the most important thing" to grasp in seeking to understand Wisdom "is that wisdom does not turn towards man in the shape of an 'It,' teaching, guidance, salvation or the like, but of a person, a summoning 'I.'"[33] As R. E. Murphy indicates, Wisdom "is the divine summons issued in and through creation, sounding through the vast realm of the created world and heard on the level of human experience."[34] Likewise, in contrast to the impression that the sages did not teach the public, C. L. Seow demonstrates that in ancient Israel "public teaching was not contradictory to the task of the sages, but integral to it." He wisely points to Proverbs 8:4 (his translation): "Unto you, O people, I call out, / my cry is to humanity."[35]

These descriptions of the task of Wisdom sound very similar to what the Fourth Evangelist has done in portraying Jesus. The Johannine Jesus launches forth in long discourses or hortatory summonses directed to more than his chosen ones. Furthermore, both Lady Wisdom and Jesus teach truth and justice (Proverbs 8; *Sentences of the Syriac Menander* 2.27–33). It is possible that the portrait of Wisdom influenced the Fourth Evangelist when he portrayed Jesus stressing that "you will know the truth, and the truth will make you free" (John 8:32). Jesus is also depicted as telling Thomas, "I am the way, and the truth, and the life" (14:6). These attributes of Jesus root Johannine Christology in wisdom traditions.

Wisdom and Jesus Promise Life and Everlasting Life

The influence of Jewish wisdom traditions on the Fourth Gospel becomes obvious when one notices how Lady Wisdom and Jesus promise life and everlasting life. According to Proverbs 8:35 Wisdom says, "whoever finds me finds life." According to Wisdom of Solomon 8:17 "with wisdom there is immortality." The one commodity — if such apparently vulgar language is permissible — offered by the Johannine community is life and eternal life (see esp. John 1:3–4). In its first edition the Fourth Gospel ended by claiming that what had been written was so that "you may have life in [Jesus'] name." Throughout the Gospel, as is well known, and in striking contrast to the Synoptics, is the promise of life and eternal life. In the first edition, and using Mosaic theology, Jesus promises Nicodemus that "as Moses lifted up the serpent in the wilderness, so must the Son of Man be lifted up, that whoever believes in him may have eternal life" (3:14–15). Jesus promises the Samaritan woman that he has living water so that all who drink of it will have "a spring of water welling up to eternal life" (4:14 RSV).

Wisdom and Jesus Bring Love and Joy

Jewish wisdom traditions are evident in the Fourth Gospel since Lady Wisdom and Jesus are depicted as bringing love and joy. According to Proverbs 8:34 the one who finds Wisdom is happy, and Lady Wisdom states, "Happy are those who keep my ways" (8:32). She is described as the Lord's daily delight (8:30), because she has been "rejoicing before him always," indeed "rejoicing in his inhabited world / and delighting in the human race" (8:31). This positive and optimistic tone is typical of Wisdom literature, and it is here that we find the greatest contrast with Jewish apocalypticism, especially its denigration of the present world. According to the Wisdom of Solomon, "the Lord of all loves her" (8:3), and in subsequent verses we are told that "friendship with her" is "pure delight" (8:18). According to *Beatitudes* (4Q525) the one who attains Wisdom is blessed and takes pleasure in her. The constant stress on Wisdom as a source of joy is one of the reasons I translate *yirat yhwh* not as "the fear of the LORD" (as in Proverbs 9:10, NRSV) but as "the awe of the LORD."[36]

No Gospel emphasizes love (*agapē*) and joy more than the Fourth Gospel.[37] Only according to it does Jesus teach a commandment, "I give you a new commandment, that you love one another ... as I have loved you" (John 13:34). Only in the Fourth Gospel does Jesus explicitly wish joy for his followers. In fact, only in the Fourth Gospel is Jesus depicted as urging his followers to have "joy" (*hē chara*). He tells his followers, "These things I have spoken to you, so that my joy may be in you, and that your joy may be full" (15:11, RSV). He promises them that their sorrow "will turn into joy" (16:20). This joy will not be ephemeral; according to the Fourth Gospel Jesus proclaims that "no one will take your joy from you" (16:22). Jesus urges his followers to ask anything from him, so that upon receiving it their "joy may be complete" (16:24). As Jesus is returning to heaven, like Wisdom in some apocalypses (esp. *1 Enoch*), he tells his Father, "These things I speak in the world, that they may have my joy fulfilled in themselves" (17:13, RSV). There should be little doubt that here again Johannine Christology has been shaped by wisdom traditions.

Wisdom and Jesus Bring Friendship with God

Jewish wisdom traditions are apparent in the Gospel of John, since Lady Wisdom and Jesus bring the greatest treasure: friendship with God. According to Wisdom of Solomon 7:27, Wisdom enters holy souls every generation "and makes them friends of God." This thought is close to the central concept in the prayer of Jesus in the Fourth Gospel. Jesus is reputed to have said, "The Father himself loves you, because you have loved me and have believed that I came from the Father" (John 16:27, RSV). His subsequent prayer is highly charged with wisdom traditions. What does Jesus pray? He prays that "they may all be one; even as you, Father, are in me, and I in you, that they also may be in us, so that the world may believe that you have sent me" (17:21, my translation).

Summary

Thinking on these six major links between Jewish wisdom traditions and the Gospel of John offers important insights. By studying the impact of wisdom on Johannine Christology it becomes clear that eternal life, justice, and righteousness are not to be understood in ethical terms or as maxims of moral theology. They are possible only because of a personal relationship to God, either through Wisdom or through Jesus Christ. Also, as in the Wisdom of Solomon, so in the Fourth Gospel there is little or no concern with resurrection after death; immortality is much rather understood as being with God permanently, beginning here and now on earth. So Jesus is reported to have said to the Samaritan woman, "Whoever drinks of the water that I shall give him will never thirst; the water that I shall give him will become in him a spring of water welling up to eternal life" (John 4:14, RSV). That is a promise for the here and now. In contrast to Paul, the author of the Fourth Gospel does not stress the transforming effects of the resurrection. In this regard he is closer to wisdom traditions than to Pauline theology.

Having surveyed these passages we have hardly exposed the full dimension of wisdom found in the Fourth Gospel. Recognizing that wisdom comes only from experiences — that is, careful reflections on what happens to us — we need to focus on one question: In what pericope did the Fourth Evangelist portray Jesus in nonmetaphorical terms as one who was wise and who had learned from his associations with others? For me that passage is John 2:23–25, in the beginning of the Gospel: "Many trusted (or believed; *episteusan*) in his name having seen the signs which he did; but Jesus did not trust himself (*episteuen auton*) to them, because he knew all and needed no one to bear witness of the human; for he knew what was in the human" (my translation). This is remarkable. Jesus did not trust himself to others, especially to those who believed in him. Why? Because he knew what was in them, what dwelled in their hearts. That means that Jesus had learned, had experienced, that he could not trust those closely associated with him. Many of us who have lived long enough have experienced just that phenomenon — those closest to us, sometimes our family members, have occasionally broken trust with us and have betrayed us. Jesus, according to the Fourth Evangelist, had also experienced this pain. But the greatness of Jesus' wisdom is that, in spite of his knowledge that his closest ones, especially Peter and Judas, would deny him or betray him, he nevertheless subsequently trusted himself to them — most impressively in the washing of their feet and in the long discourses of John 15–17.

Wisdom Traditions and Christology in John's Prologue

The evidence that the Fourth Gospel portrays Jesus in light of wisdom tradition is proved beyond any doubt by examination of the prologue (John 1:1–18). Like the *Odes of Solomon,* the prologue is a Logos hymn that was probably recited liturgically in the Johannine community. The evangelist chose to prefix his Gospel with this hymn, most likely to stress the point he had already presented: Jesus can be understood as Wisdom. In the prologue, the links with wisdom traditions are both clear and outstanding.

Wisdom and Logos Antedate Creation

According to Proverbs 8:22–29, Wisdom was created "at the beginning"; and according to Sirach 24:9, Wisdom was "in the beginning." This concept surely resonates in the first words of the Fourth Gospel: "In the beginning was the Logos." Such thoughts are said of Wisdom by Jews for centuries before the composition of the Fourth Gospel and long after it. The preexistence of Christ is a feature unique to the Fourth Gospel among the intracanonical Gospels, appearing elsewhere in the New Testament only in Colossians 1:15–20 and in Hebrews 1:1–3. The Fourth Evangelist frequently portrays Jesus as one who is preexistent. He states that Christ antedates Abraham (John 8:58) and articulates in the very beginning of the Gospel, through words uttered by one sent from God (namely John the Baptizer; 1:6) the preexistence of Christ. John the Baptizer affirms about Jesus (all quotations from Revised Standard Version):

> This was he of whom I said, "He who comes after me ranks before me, for he was before me."   — John 1:15

> He who comes after me.   — John 1:27

> This is he of whom I said, "After me comes a man who ranks before me, for he was before me."   — John 1:30

Brown rightly states that these passages "once associated with the beginning of the ministry of Jesus" appear in the final edition of the Fourth Gospel to articulate "the incarnation of the pre-existent Word."[38] In the Fourth Gospel John the Baptizer is cast not as he probably was; that is, as a prophet proclaiming the coming judgment. He is cast in the light of Johannine Christology. He is Jesus' precursor and herald. In the words of Brown he is "an incipient Christian," and in the view of G. Stanton he is a "Christian evangelist."[39] In any case, John the Baptizer emphasizes that Jesus precedes him. That means that Jesus, as the Logos, was preexistent, like Wisdom.

Wisdom and Logos Are the Agents of Creation

According to the Wisdom of Solomon, Wisdom is the "fashioner of all things" (7:22; cf. 8:6). Centuries later, for example, in the *Hellenistic Synagogal Prayers* a Jew explained that Wisdom was the means by which God created and gave order (3.19). Later in the same collection a Christian interpolated the thought that Jesus is not only the Son, but also the Word and Wisdom, the firstborn:

> The one who brought everything into being out of non-being, through your only Son,

and gave him birth before all the ages,
by purpose, and power, and unmediated goodness —
an only Son, a divine Word, a living Wisdom,
a firstborn of all creation,
a messenger of your great purpose.
> — *Hellenistic Synagogal Prayers* 12.9–10[40]

This learned Christian, who edited this earlier Jewish prayer, knew well both Wisdom literature and the Fourth Gospel and presented Christ in the light of both. Centuries earlier, most likely in the Johannine community, a Jew who had become a Christian composed a poetic hymn that conveyed a similar thought:

> The Father of knowledge
> is the Word of knowledge.
> He who created wisdom
> is wiser than his works.
> — *Odes of Solomon* 7.7–8

This poetic genius brought together the concepts of God the Father, the Word, and Wisdom and rearticulated the heart of Judaism and Christianity: monotheism. Reviewing these texts brings home the dimension of Wisdom in John 1:3: "All things were made through him (the Logos), and without him was not anything made that was made."

As W. Zimmerli and Murphy emphasize, "Wisdom theology is creation theology."[41] According to Proverbs 8:30 Wisdom is an *amon*, which seems to mean "crafts[wo]man." One of the features of Johannine theology is that eschatology (i.e., concern for the end of time) is deemphasized in favor of protology (i.e., study of the beginnings of time and space). Like some traditions attributed to Wisdom, the Logos is the sole agent of creation.

Wisdom and Logos Are with God in Heaven

Both wisdom tradition and the Logos hymn emphasize that Wisdom or the Logos is with God in heaven:

> All wisdom is from the Lord,
> and with him it remains forever.
> . . . .
> Wisdom was created before all other things,
> and prudent understanding from eternity.
> — Sirach 1:1, 4

According to the Wisdom of Solomon, Wisdom "sits by" God's throne (9:4); she is sent forth from "the holy heavens, and from the throne" of God (9:10). Stunningly similar words are attributed to the Logos: "In the beginning was the Logos, and the Logos was with (or before) God" (John 1:1). According to Sirach 24:2 Wisdom is "in the assembly of the Most High," an idea that is also adumbrated in John 1:1: the Logos is *pros ton theon,* usually translated "with God" but literally "before God." The Hebrew equivalent is *lipne elohim,* a technical means of referring to the place of the angels, especially the archangels, who minister *in the presence of* or *before* God in the heavenly courts. Having made the point that the Logos was serving like an archangel in God's court, the author of the Logos hymn wants to stress that the Logos is, like Wisdom, above the archangels. Thus, he adds immediately *kai theos ēn ho logos,* which is not easily translated into English, although it is usually rendered "and the Word was God." The function of these words cannot be to state unqualifiedly that Logos is God, since the author has just stated that the Logos administered before God. Their function is to warn against any paradigmatic distinction between Logos and God. And with that theological move the author is again indebted to Wisdom literature. Like Wisdom, the Logos is in the heavenly court before God; but unlike Wisdom, the Logos is to be identified with God.

Wisdom and Logos Bring Life and Light

The author of Proverbs 8:35 has Wisdom state, "Whoever finds me finds life." According to Ecclesiastes 2:13 "wisdom excels folly as light excels darkness." The author of the Wisdom of

Solomon explains that Wisdom excels every constellation in the heavens, and "compared with the light she is found to be superior" (7:29). Running throughout all the wisdom books is the constant theme that without Wisdom there is darkness and death; only with her is there light and life. Such ideas obviously helped shape Johannine Christology, especially the explanation that in the Logos "was life, and the life was the light of all people" (John 1:4). Even more strikingly related to Wisdom — especially the tradition that Wisdom enters into holy souls (Wisdom of Solomon 7:27) — is the claim that the Logos is "the true light that enlightens every person coming into the world" (John 1:9, my translation).

Wisdom and Logos Could Not Find a Home on Earth

As we have shown earlier, the *Apocalypse of Enoch* explains that Wisdom could not find a home on earth (*1 Enoch* 42). At this stage in our study, it becomes more evident that such a concept was in the mind of the author: "He came to his own home, but his own people did not receive him" (John 1:11, my translation).

Wisdom and Logos Are Portrayed as God Tenting among God's People

In Sirach 24:8 we find the following interesting passage from the mouth of Lady Wisdom:

> Then the Creator of all things gave me a command,
> and my Creator chose the place for my tent (*skēnēn*).

This concept most likely shaped the prologue of the Fourth Gospel in John 1:14: "The Logos became flesh and dwelled among us." The second verb, *eskēnōsen*, literally means "tented"; hence, Wisdom is said to be given a tent by God. It is *prima facie* evident that here also wisdom tradition helped couch the presentation of the Logos who tented among humans. These observations lead me to agree wholeheartedly with R. Bultmann's conclusion that "there can be no doubt, in fact, that a connection exists between the Judaic Wisdom myth and the Johannine Prologue."[42] One can easily imagine why W. F. Howard suggests that we should see 1:14 as an insertion in a pre-Christian hymn that was apparently authored in praise of Wisdom.[43]

As M. W. G. Stibbe states, the "most probable intertextual background"[44] for the concept of Word, or Logos, in the prologue "lies in the Jewish mythology of personified Wisdom."[45] The author of this portion of the Fourth Gospel portrays "Jesus as the creative and life-giving Word, [and] the narrator creates an intertextual relationship between the protagonist and the figure of Wisdom."[46] Thus, like Wisdom, the Word or Logos antedates creation, is with (or before) God in heaven, is the agent of creation, and brings life and light into the world and into the hearts of humans. Like Wisdom, the Word or Logos according to the prologue tented among humans; but, according to the following chapters in the Fourth Gospel, Jesus, who is never explicitly identified as Logos, eventually returned to heaven to be with God his Father.

Summary

As we imagine the composition of the Fourth Gospel within the Johannine community, especially from the first edition (perhaps) in the late sixties to the second edition in the late nineties, we should not imagine the Jews in the community searching for links or parallels between Christ and Wisdom. They were not like a young research student or professor who reads the documents mentioned above looking for possible parallels. The Jews who gave us the Fourth Gospel were highly educated. They represented some of the best minds in the first century C.E. They knew the wisdom books. These were sacred. They were present in their community as scrolls. For most of them the original languages were their own native tongues, Hebrew and Greek. The wisdom traditions were read not as something old but as something refreshingly new.

Proverbs, Sirach, the Wisdom of Solomon, and Baruch were sacred scriptures. They breathed the world of wisdom and these texts were committed to memory by many of the Johannine Jews. Hence, when they came to think and discuss the meaning of Jesus' life and teachings, they expressed their thoughts in terms of the wisdom traditions that had been dear to them and their ancestors. Wisdom was indeed one of the traditions that shaped Johannine Christology.

What is unique about my work presented here? It begins with the first edition of the Fourth Gospel and only subsequently turns to the second edition that contained the prologue and Logos hymn. The search for a better understanding of wisdom's influences on Johannine Christology must not begin and be grounded in the Logos hymn. It was a prefixed work of genius, but it depends on the Gospel that preceded it and now ironically follows it. Also, I included in my survey many Jewish wisdom writings that are usually not mentioned in the discussions; among these are the nonsectarian wisdom traditions found in the Qumran caves. Finally, I pointed out numerous parallels that have been overlooked.

I mentioned only in passing the important books on wisdom and Johannine Christology. Now, I can explain how and in what ways I agree or disagree with colleagues who are also interested in this intriguing area of reflection and research. I shall limit myself to brief reflections on only four books that appeared recently.

In *Sophia and the Johannine Jesus,* M. Scott seems primarily interested in women in the New Testament. He rightly stresses that Sophia (Wisdom) is primarily a personification in Proverbs and perhaps Sirach, but in the Wisdom of Solomon, in which she reaches her highest development among the parabiblical books, she is certainly more than a personification. She is, in Scott's words, "effectively God in feminine form."[47] The focus of my study has, of course, been the latter part of the first century C.E. It concerns the time after Philo of Alexandria, who worked in Egypt at the beginning of the first century, and in whose work Wisdom is most likely hypostatic. I am convinced that by the end of the first century C.E. we should recognize that Wisdom is portrayed as a hypostasis in some Jewish groups and that we should be open to the probability that these Jews may have influenced the Johannine community. Scott shows how and in what ways Logos and Wisdom before the composition of the Fourth Gospel "had become more or less synonymous in at least some areas of Jewish thought."[48] He concludes, perhaps without the necessary qualifications, "that the Logos of the Prologue is none other than Sophia."[49] Also he exaggerates the influence of wisdom on the Gospel of John not only when he claims that the body of the Gospel embellishes the picture of Jesus as Sophia incarnate,[50] but also when he contends that "the Gospel is a presentation of the life and ministry of Jesus Sophia."[51] As seen above, similarities and dissimilarities may be found between Lady Wisdom and Johannine theology.

Scott astutely confronts the question why the Fourth Evangelist does not simply have Jesus state, "I am Wisdom." His main answer is that Jesus was an incarnate male and Sophia is distinctly portrayed as a very attractive female. The answer is appealing and tends to vitiate his hypothesis that in the Fourth Gospel the Logos, or Jesus, is simply Sophia.

A book dedicated more to the prologue than to the issue of Wisdom and Christology is C. A. Evans's insightful *Word and Glory*. In this book Evans obviously must include his reflection on the link between Johannine Christology and Wisdom. In line with established scholars like M.-É. Boismard, J. D. G. Dunn, J. Jeremias, B. Lindars, M. de Jonge, and E. Ruckstuhl, Evans concludes that "the closest parallels to Johannine thought, particularly with respect to its Christology, are to be found in the Old Testament Wisdom tradition."[52] I demonstrated that Evans is right on target.

In *Moses or Jesus*, M.-É. Boismard, a gifted exegete internationally celebrated for thirty years as an expert on the Fourth Gospel, presents his mature reflections on Johannine Christology. He is persuaded that the Fourth Evangelist presents Jesus as "the Wisdom of God" in the world. Jesus is himself "the Wisdom and Law which speaks to men to tell them how they have to act in order to please God."[53] Boismard argues that the Fourth Evangelist "speaks of Jesus in the same way as the Wisdom books speak of Wisdom; better still, he puts in Jesus' mouth the words uttered by Wisdom in the sapiential books."[54] For the Fourth Evangelist Jesus "was not simply a prophet," he was much more: "In him was incarnated the Wisdom of God that the sapiential books said must come into the world to teach men how to live in accordance with the will of God."[55] Boismard does not exaggerate the importance of Wisdom on Johannine Christology; he also points out that the Fourth Evangelist portrays Jesus as "the Prophet *par excellence*, the new Moses announced by Deuteronomy 18:18."[56] This balance is attractive in Boismard's work.

In 1995 B. Witherington III published a commentary on the Fourth Gospel that he entitled *John's Wisdom*. He correctly reports that the "Wisdom character and background of the Logos hymn has long been recognized."[57] He doubts that the Fourth Gospel uses Logos instead of Sophia "because Jesus was a male."[58] Witherington rightly points out that Logos, or Word, is synonymous with Wisdom according to Wisdom of Solomon 9:1–2 (my translation):

> O God of my ancestors and Lord of mercy,
> who made all things by your Word,
> and formed humankind by your Wisdom.

He also points to Wisdom of Solomon 18:14–16, which depicts a personified and perhaps hypostatic Word:[59]

> For while gentle silence enveloped all things,
> . . . .
> Your all-powerful Word leaped from heaven, from the royal
>   throne,
> . . . .
> A stern warrior carrying the sharp sword of your authentic
>   command, and stood.

In this passage the Word leaps, was on the throne, and is depicted as a stern warrior brandishing a sword. The distinction between personification and hypostatization is evident in this passage. The actions of Wisdom are not grounded in the meaning of a concept like Word; that is, the actions or descriptions of the subject do not derive from the etymological meaning of the root concept. For example, according to the root meaning of the noun, a word can be said to come forth and be heard but it cannot be said to leap from the royal throne or carry a sharp sword and stand. Thus, we have in the Wisdom of Solomon the concept of a hypostatized Word.[60] Of course, as I stated earlier, this concept of hypostatization is not to be linked conceptually with the discussions over Christology in the fourth or fifth centuries C.E.

Another passage regarding Wisdom and Word has eluded the experts.[61] In *The Preparation for the Gospel* Eusebius, the first great Christian historian, states that "the oracles of the Hebrews" accentuate the existence of "the Being of the God of the universe." He also mentions "a second Being and divine power, which subsisted as the first beginning of all originated things and was originated from the first cause, calling it Word, and 'Wisdom, and Power of God.' "[62] Quoting Proverbs 8, Wisdom of Solomon 6–8, the Psalms, and Genesis, Eusebius clarifies that Jews linked Wisdom with Word and that both were hypostatic beings that existed from the very beginning. Citing the Prophets, in which the word of Yahweh is sent to them, he states that the Jews interpret "and the Lord said" (*wayyomer yhwh*) and "thus says the Lord" (*koh amar yhwh*) to denote the sending of the Word through the prophets to humans: "This divine Word in various ways is sent from the Father for the salvation of mankind" (*Preparation for the Gospel* 7.12d). Citing an otherwise unknown passage in Philo, Eusebius refers to the preexistence of the Word: "From the womb I begat thee before the morning star" (7.12d). It is wise to heed these reports by Eusebius. We have no way of knowing how much is now lost but was once available to

Jews before the time of the final editing of the Fourth Gospel (circa 95 C.E.).

How does Witherington interpret Wisdom of Solomon 9 and 18? He concludes that these passages explain why Logos instead of the feminine Wisdom appears in the Fourth Gospel; that is, Logos and Sophia were already identified in early Jewish theology. This is an important contribution, but we must not forget Scott's insight that the main reason for the depiction of Jesus as Logos and not as Wisdom is because Jesus was male. In my judgment, we are not faced with an either-or; rather, both interpretations are helpful. Beginning with the body of the Gospel in which Jesus is clearly a male (Jesus son of Joseph) and subsequently hearing the tonal accents of the prologue, especially John 1:14, it is clear to me that the Fourth Evangelist inherited the concept of Wisdom as a female person. In some texts she is already associated with Word, which has also, like Wisdom, become a hypostasis. Then, with the light provided by these traditions and many others, it seems obvious that the Fourth Evangelist portrayed the Logos in harmony with his focused story of the life of a Jewish male.

Finally, why does Witherington call his commentary *John's Wisdom?* He is convinced that "the great debt to the Wisdom tradition that this Gospel reflects has been under-appreciated."[63] Hence, his commentary on the Fourth Gospel is intended "to read this Gospel in the light of Jewish and early Christian wisdom material."[64] I am not convinced that the wisdom-tradition influence on the Fourth Gospel is underappreciated. In 1917 J. R. Harris emphasized this point, and it has been developed by Brown, Dodd, Dunn, and others.[65] It is a pity that in 1995 Witherington did not benefit from or cite (as did Scott in 1992) M. E. Willett's *Wisdom Christology in the Fourth Gospel*,[66] which was available in 1985. Nevertheless, Witherington is correct to point out that the wisdom tradition has shaped virtually every section of the Fourth Gospel.

Conclusion

We have seen that two contradictory ideas about the abode of
Wisdom were held by Jews before the destruction of 70 C.E.
The apocalypses, especially *1 Enoch* 42, stressed that Wisdom
did not find a home on the earth. Studying wisdom apocalypsology we can better perceive how the author of the Fourth
Gospel developed his portrayal of Jesus; he is the one who
is from above and is only on his way back to the Father.[67] It
is evident also why the Fourth Evangelist removes the suffering and prayer in Gethsemane and shifts the cry on the
cross from "my God, my God, why have you forsaken me" to
"it is finished."[68] From beginning to end of the Fourth Gospel, Jesus is portrayed as one moving gloriously toward full
glory so that he will be "lifted up" on the cross — that is,
crucifixion becomes exaltation.[69] It also becomes more apparent why some scholars, especially E. Käsemann, think that
the Christology of the Fourth Gospel was incipiently docetic.
The source for this tendency may be the power of wisdom
theology on Johannine Christology; and in that inheritance is
the glory of Wisdom attributed to Jesus. As Käsemann states,
"No other Gospel narrates as impressively as John the confrontation of the world and of the believers with the glory of
Jesus, even in the passion story."[70]

Wisdom literature, beginning with Sirach 24 and Baruch
3–4, stressed that Wisdom found a place on earth in Torah.
Thus in line with these Jews and with early rabbinic sages,
the author of the Fourth Gospel could develop something
new — he portrayed Jesus, as Wisdom, on earth, teaching
and exhorting "the sons of light" to return to the Father. The
Johannine community can say, "We have beheld his glory,
glory as of the only Son from the Father" (John 1:14, RSV). In
this verse wisdom and apocalypticism meet.

Thus, the Fourth Gospel is influenced by wisdom and
apocalypsology, but the product is neither a wisdom tract nor
an apocalyptic work. The Fourth Gospel, we must not forget,
was influenced by many aspects of Judaism, including the

Dead Sea Scrolls and the Old Testament. The beginning of the Fourth Gospel, *en archē* (John 1:1), is borrowed directly from the Septuagint version of Genesis 1:1: *en archē*. The present research brings into the foreground the obvious fact that the Fourth Gospel is not a Greek philosophical work. It is a Jewish composition, profoundly influenced by the advanced and elevated thoughts developed in the Old Testament and in the Jewish literature that post-dated it. When we remember that probably Pharisees, Samaritans, and Essenes among other Jewish groups became members of the Johannine community, it is no wonder that the Fourth Gospel reflects the achievement of numerous highly educated and gifted Jews, most likely among them *khakamim* or "wise ones." Wisdom certainly helped in the development of Johannine Christology. I am in full agreement with D. M. Smith's conclusion that "if one asks where the idea that God uses a mediator in creation, and ultimately in redemption, originates, an important answer may be found in the biblically based personification of wisdom."[71] It is thus clear that wisdom influenced the presentation of Jesus in the Gospel (John 1:19–21) and in the prologue. Recent research makes it abundantly clear that we do not need to look beyond the borders of early Jewish theology in order to find the source from which the Fourth Evangelist developed much of his Christology.[72]

Is wisdom the key to Johannine Christology? W. Grundmann answers "yes" when he claims that the Logos idea is the foundational thought (*Grundaussage*) upon which all other elements of the Christology are based and that this Christology is not primarily influenced by Greek philosophy but by the wisdom tradition.[73] Influenced by Bultmann, W. Loader is convinced that the key or center of Johannine Christology is the sending formula, which is associated with Wisdom.[74] I doubt that the metaphor of a mysterious lock to which a key can be found is appropriate for comprehending Johannine Christology. Sonship is so important in Johannine Christology, and this concept develops out of many early strains of Old Testament theology, including the royal enthronement

psalms, which depict the king becoming the son of God
(Psalms 2:7). While wisdom is one of the major sources for
Johannine Christology, it is not the only source.

We must, furthermore, also be aware that the Fourth Gospel does not contain a claim that "Christ [is] the wisdom of
God" (1 Corinthians 1:24). In fact the word *sophia* (wisdom)
does not appear in the Fourth Gospel, although it is found
once in Mark, three times in Matthew,[75] six times in Luke,
and seventeen times in 1 Corinthians.

These statistics inform us that wisdom theology is not
the primary key to Johannine Christology. It was shaped
by many facets in early Judaism, notably the thoughts and
technical terms found in the Dead Sea Scrolls. As close to
anything in the wisdom tradition is a passage in the *Rule of
the Community* that sounds much like the opening of the prologue: "By his (God's) knowledge all shall occur. All which
is occurring he establishes by his design, and without him
(nothing) shall work" (1QS 11.11).[76] This caveat should not
diminish our discovery that the author of the Fourth Gospel is a Jew who took many of the words and descriptions
attributed to Wisdom and transferred them to the Logos
and to Jesus, whom he proclaimed to be the Christ. After
the composition of the Fourth Gospel, Christians took a Jewish psalmbook and interpolated it under the influence of the
Fourth Gospel. One of the purposes of the Christian redactor was to identify Christ with Wisdom. I thus conclude by
citing this hymn:

> And you appointed festivals for (the) gladdening of our souls,
>   so that we may come into remembrance of the Wisdom
>   created by you;
> *how for us he submitted to birth, that (birth) through a woman;*
> *(how) he appeared in (this) life, having demonstrated himself in (his)*
>   *baptism;*
> *how he who appeared is God and man;*
> *(how) he suffered for us with your consent,*
> *and (how) he died and arose by your strength.*
>   — *Hellenistic Synagogal Prayers* 5.3–6[77]

Here in this hymn we find an identification of Jesus with Wisdom, and the author of this hymn is clearly under the influence of the Fourth Gospel.

In summation, the Fourth Evangelist presented the life and teachings of Jesus according to set paradigms and refined symbols and motifs. It represented his Christology, which was shaped by many aspects of Jewish theology. One of the most prominent influences among them was wisdom. As in the apocalyptic view of wisdom, Jesus comes from above and returns to the world above because this is an evil world ruled by Satan. Like Jewish Wisdom literature, Jesus calls all to him and instructs them concerning the way, the truth, and the life. Like Wisdom he personifies these virtues. Like Wisdom he brings joy to those who know him and offers them life, indeed eternal life. All of this transpires in the body of the Gospel — from John 1:19 to the end.

The prologue was clearly added later and may well have been, like the *Odes of Solomon,* one of the hymns recited within the Johannine community (with the caveat that the *Odes of Solomon* in the judgment of most critics postdates the Logos hymn by decades). According to the prologue (as in the *Odes of Solomon*), Jesus, as the Logos, is portrayed as Wisdom, existing from the beginning of time and space. He is superior to the archangels in the heavenly chambers, and like them he is before God serving him. Like Wisdom he is radiant with glory and grace. Because the Fourth Evangelist began with a story of the life of a Jewish male, Jesus son of Joseph, he cannot portray Jesus as Sophia (*hē sophia*), which is a feminine grammatical form and concept. Logos, as Sophia, as Jesus Christ, is the one who transcends time and space; he was before Abraham and from the beginning. He alone is from above and returns there to prepare a place for all those who are wise enough to hear and heed his voice.

Notes

1. See esp. D. J. Harrington, *Wisdom Texts from Qumran* (New York: Routledge, 1996).

2. See esp. J. L. Crenshaw, *Old Testament Wisdom: An Introduction* (Atlanta: John Knox, 1981).

3. The translation of *4 Maccabees* is from H. Anderson, "4 Maccabees," in *The Old Testament Pseudepigrapha* (ed. J. H. Charlesworth; New York: Doubleday, 1985), 2.531–64.

4. L. G. Perdue, *Wisdom and Creation: The Theology of Wisdom Literature* (Nashville: Abingdon, 1994), 78.

5. I tend to agree with C. Westermann, against G. von Rad, H. J. Hermisson, and H. D. Preuss, that the roots of Israelite wisdom are found in preliterary folk cultures. See C. Westermann, *Roots of Wisdom: The Oldest Proverbs of Israel and Other Peoples* (trans. J. D. Charles; Louisville: Westminster John Knox, 1995), 4.

6. See R. B. Y. Scott, *The Way of Wisdom in the Old Testament* (New York: Macmillan, 1971), 6.

7. Here I differ slightly with my esteemed colleague R. E. Murphy. I am convinced that postexilic Judaism and Second Temple Judaism cannot always be labeled "monotheistic" — some theological reflections are clearly henotheistic. Also, I am persuaded that in the centuries before the first century C.E. there are Jewish developments of wisdom beyond those of a personified Wisdom (as in Proverbs); but these developments postdate the wisdom books in the Old Testament. See R. E. Murphy, *The Tree of Life: An Exploration of Biblical Wisdom Literature* (Anchor Bible Reference Library; New York: Doubleday, 1990), 133. I fully agree with Murphy that in the Hebrew Bible and early Jewish sources "no personification [is] comparable to that of wisdom"; idem, "The Personification of Wisdom," in *Wisdom in Ancient Israel: Essays in Honour of J. A. Emerton* (ed. J. Day, R. P. Gordon, and H. G. M. Williamson; Cambridge: Cambridge University Press, 1995), 222.

8. In this depiction of Wisdom, notice the importance given to "glory." I will pick this theme up later.

9. Unless otherwise noted, all translations of the Old Testament, Old Testament Apocrypha, and New Testament are from the New Revised Standard Version.

10. In these christological reflections I side with R. E. Brown, R. T. Fortna, H. Ridderbos, J. L Martyn, and U. C. von Wahlde (*pace* W. Langbrandtner).

11. Translations of *1 Enoch* are from E. Isaac, "1 (Ethiopic Apocalypse of) Enoch," in *The Old Testament Pseudepigrapha* (ed. J. H. Charlesworth; New York: Doubleday, 1983), 1.5–89.

12. M. E. Willett also points out the pervasive thematic influence of Wisdom in the Gospel of John; see his *Wisdom Christology in the Fourth Gospel* (San Francisco: Mellen, 1992), 49–126.

13. For Hebrew text and translation, see J. H. Charlesworth, "The Qumran Beatitudes (4Q525) and the New Testament (Mt 5:3–11, Lk 6:2–26)," *Revue d'histoire et de philosophie religieuses* 80 (2000): 13–35.

14. For the context and the Hebrew, see S. R. Hirsch, *Chapters of the Fathers* (Jerusalem: Feldheim, 1989), 28–29.

15. This is part of Wisdom's speech.

16. The links with Wisdom are implicit.

17. Translations of the *Odes of Solomon* are from J. H. Charlesworth, "Odes of Solomon," in *The Old Testament Pseudepigrapha* (ed. J. H. Charlesworth; New York: Doubleday, 1985), 2.725–71.

18. According to *1 Enoch (Ethiopic Apocalypse)* 48–49 and 52, the Elect One seems to be indistinct from and even identical with "his Messiah." In 53.6 the Righteous One is clearly the Elect One. In *1 Enoch* 62 the Elect One seems clearly to be identical with that (or the) Son of Man. According to *1 Enoch* 71 Enoch is "that Son of Man." For full discussions of the relationship between the Son of Man and the Messiah as well as other figures, see the contributions by J. H. Charlesworth, M. Black, and J. C. VanderKam in *The Messiah* (ed. J. H. Charlesworth; Minneapolis: Fortress, 1992).

19. G. von Rad, *Wisdom in Israel* (trans. J. D. Martin; London: SCM, 1972; repr. London: SCM/Valley Forge, Pa.: Trinity, 1993).

20. R. A. Coughenour, "The Wisdom Stance of Enoch's Redactor," *Journal for the Study of Judaism in the Persian, Hellenistic, and Roman Periods* 13 (1982): 47–55; the quotation is on 47; cf. 55.

21. "Apocalypsology" is a neologism indicating apocalyptic reflections on theology.

22. A. S. van der Woude, "Wisdom at Qumran," in *Wisdom in Ancient Israel: Essays in Honour of J. A. Emerton* (ed. J. Day, R. P. Gordon, and H. G. M. Williamson; Cambridge: Cambridge University Press, 1995), 252.

23. D. Winston, *Philo of Alexandria* (New York: Paulist, 1981), 94–95.

24. See F. Dexinger in *The Samaritans* (ed. A. D. Crown; Tübingen: Mohr [Siebeck], 1989), 275; idem, *Der Taheb: Ein "messianischer" Heilsbringer der Samaritaner* (KAIROS 3; Salzburg: Müller, 1986), esp. 13–17.

25. See J. Fossum, "Samaritan Sects and Movements," in *The Samaritans* (ed. A. D. Crown; Tübingen: Mohr [Siebeck], 1989), 362.

26. It is also possible, perhaps probable, that the author of the Fourth Gospel knew and inherited the additions to Sirach 24:17 found

in some Greek manuscripts. These contain the emphasis on love (*agapēseōs*) and being named by him (*tois legomenois hyp' autou*), *topoi* found in the Fourth Gospel.

27. Translation from A. Y. Collins, "Aristobulus," in *The Old Testament Pseudepigrapha* (ed. J. H. Charlesworth; New York: Doubleday, 1985), 2.841. I have capitalized Wisdom because she is said to hold a lantern.

28. The image of a mirror is found in the New Testament only in 1 Corinthians 13:12 and James 1:23.

29. See J. Kuhl, *Die Sendung Jesu und der Kirche nach dem Johannes-Evangelium* (Studia Instituti Missiologici Societatis Verbi Divini 11; St. Augustin/Siegsburg, Washington: Steyler, 1967), 53–55.

30. See P. W. Meyer, " 'The Father': The Presentation of God in the Fourth Gospel," in *Exploring the Gospel of John: In Honor of D. Moody Smith* (ed. R. A. Culpepper and C. C. Black; Louisville: Westminster John Knox, 1996), 255–73.

31. The Greek adverb denotes primarily "from above," but it also means "again." The double entendre is intended by the evangelist, as he and the author of the *Odes of Solomon* are fond of paronomasia.

32. H. Ridderbos, *The Gospel of John* (trans. J. Vriend; Grand Rapids: Eerdmans, 1997), 34.

33. G. von Rad, *Old Testament Theology*, vol. 1: *The Theology of Israel's Historical Traditions* (trans. D. M. G. Stalker; New York: Harper & Row, 1962), 444.

34. Murphy, *Tree of Life*, 138.

35. C. L. Seow, " 'Beyond Them, My Son, Be Warned': The Epilogue of Qoheleth Revisited," in *Wisdom, You Are My Sister: Studies in Honor of Roland E. Murphy, O.Carm.* (ed. M. L. Barré; Catholic Biblical Quarterly Monograph Series 29; Washington, D.C.: Catholic Biblical Association of America, 1997), 128.

36. The triliteral root behind this feminine noun, *yr'*, means both "to fear" and "to stand in awe before" someone, especially God; see Psalms 33:8. For a study of Jewish wisdom and the world religions, see J. Eaton, *The Contemplative Face of Old Testament Wisdom in the Context of World Religions* (London: SCM/Philadelphia: Trinity, 1989).

37. Greek *agapē* (love) appears once in Matthew and Luke, never in Mark, and seven times in the Gospel of John. The Greek word *chara* (joy) appears six times in Matthew, once in Mark, eight times in Luke, and nine times in the Gospel of John.

38. R. E. Brown, *The Birth of the Messiah: A Commentary on the Infancy Narratives in the Gospels of Matthew and Luke* (2d ed.; Anchor Bible Reference Library; New York: Doubleday, 1993), 284.

39. Ibid., 284–85. G. Stanton, *Gospel Truth? New Light on Jesus and the Gospels* (Valley Forge: Trinity, 1995), 166.

40. The translation is from D. R. Darnell, "Hellenistic Synagogal Prayers," in *The Old Testament Pseudepigrapha* (ed. J. H. Charlesworth; New York: Doubleday, 1985), 2.671–97.

41. Murphy, *Tree of Life*, 118.

42. R. Bultmann, *The Gospel of John: A Commentary* (trans. G. R. Beasley-Murray; Oxford: Blackwell, 1971), 22.

43. W. F. Howard, *Christianity according to St. John* (London: Duckworth, 1943), 51.

44. For the definition and discussion of intertextuality, see the articles, including my own, in *The Quest for Context and Meaning: Studies in Biblical Intertextuality in Honor of James A. Sanders* (ed. C. A. Evans and S. Talmon; Biblical Interpretation 28; Leiden: Brill, 1997).

45. M. W. G. Stibbe, *John* (Readings: A New Biblical Commentary; Sheffield: JSOT Press, 1993), 23.

46. Ibid.

47. M. Scott, *Sophia and the Johannine Jesus* (Journal for the Study of the New Testament Supplement 71; Sheffield: Sheffield Academic Press, 1992), 77.

48. Ibid., 94.

49. Ibid., 113.

50. Ibid., 159.

51. Ibid., 171.

52. C. A. Evans, *Word and Glory: On the Exegetical and Theological Background of John's Prologue* (Journal for the Study of the New Testament Supplement 89; Sheffield: Sheffield Academic Press, 1993), 83. For bibliographical details on the works of scholars mentioned, see 83–84.

53. M.-É. Boismard, *Moses or Jesus: An Essay in Johannine Christology* (trans. B. T. Viviano; Minneapolis: Fortress, 1993), 70.

54. Ibid., 72.

55. Ibid., 132–33.

56. Ibid., 132.

57. B. Witherington III, *John's Wisdom: A Commentary on the Fourth Gospel* (Louisville: Westminster/John Knox, 1995), 52. See also idem, *Jesus the Sage: The Pilgrimage of Wisdom* (Minneapolis: Fortress, 1994).

58. Witherington, *John's Wisdom*, 53.

59. The translation is based on the New Revised Standard Version, but the capitalization and arrangement are mine.

60. For more reflections on hypostatization, see J. H. Charlesworth, "The Jewish Roots of Christology: The Discovery of the Hypostatic Voice," *Scottish Journal of Theology* 39 (1986): 19–41.

61. The paronomasia may be appreciated by the astute reader who knows the symbol for the Fourth Gospel.

62. Eusebius, *The Preparation for the Gospel* 7.12d; see Eusebius, *The Preparation for the Gospel* (trans. E. H. Gifford; Oxford: Clarendon, 1903; repr. Grand Rapids: Baker, 1981), 2.320a.

63. Witherington, *John's Wisdom*, vii.

64. Ibid.

65. J. R. Harris, *The Origin of the Prologue to St. John's Gospel* (Cambridge: Cambridge University Press, 1917); R. E. Brown, *The Gospel according to John* (Garden City: Doubleday, 1966), 1.cxxii–cxxv; C. H. Dodd, *The Interpretation of the Fourth Gospel* (Cambridge: Cambridge University Press, 1953), 274–77; J. D. G. Dunn, *Christology in the Making* (London: SCM, 1980), 161–205.

66. Willett's work is a 1985 Ph.D. dissertation from Southern Baptist Theological Seminary, later published as *Wisdom Christology in the Fourth Gospel* (cited above).

67. To a certain extent the thought is reminiscent of the expansion in the *Gospel of Nicodemus*, according to which Pilate asks, "Is there no wisdom on earth?" The Johannine community could reply that Jesus, Wisdom, had returned above.

68. C. Cory claims to have found a story about Wisdom's "rescue" in John 7–8 and suggests that study of the full influence of wisdom on the Fourth Gospel may help us better understand the Fourth Evangelist's passion story; "Wisdom's Rescue: A New Reading of the Tabernacles Discourse (John 7:1–8:59)," *Journal of Biblical Literature* 116 (1997): 95–116.

69. See F. J. Moloney, *Glory Not Dishonor: Reading John 13–21* (Minneapolis: Fortress, 1998).

70. E. Käsemann, *The Testament of Jesus according to John 17* (trans. G. Krodel; Philadelphia: Fortress, 1968), 6–7.

71. D. M. Smith, *The Theology of the Gospel of John* (Cambridge: Cambridge University Press, 1995), 18.

72. For a similar conclusion, see Scott, *Sophia and the Johannine Jesus*, 28.

73. W. Grundmann, *Der Zeuge der Wahrheit: Grundzüge der Christologie des Johannesevangeliums* (Berlin: Evangelische Verlag, 1985).

74. W. Loader, *The Christology of the Fourth Gospel: Structure and Issues* (Beiträge zur biblischen Exegese und Theologie; Berlin/New York: Lang, 1992).

75. See especially the important book by C. M. Deutsch entitled *Lady Wisdom, Jesus, and the Sages* (Valley Forge, Pa.: Trinity, 1996).

76. See J. H. Charlesworth, ed., et al., *The Dead Sea Scrolls: Hebrew, Aramaic, and Greek Texts with English Translations,* vol. 1: *Rule of the Community and Related Documents* (Princeton Theological Seminary Dead Sea Scrolls Project 1; Tübingen: Mohr [Siebeck]/Louisville: Westminster John Knox, 1994), 48–49.

77. Italic type indicates Christian interpolation.

Selected Bibliography

Ashton, J. (ed.). *The Interpretation of John.* Issues in Religion and Theology 9. Philadelphia: Fortress/London: SPCK, 1986.

Barré, M. L. (ed.). *Wisdom, You Are My Sister: Studies in Honor of Roland E. Murphy, O.Carm.* Catholic Biblical Quarterly Monograph Series 29. Washington, D.C.: Catholic Biblical Association of America, 1997.

Barrett, C. K. *The Gospel according to St. John: An Introduction with Commentary and Notes on the Greek Text.* 2d edition. London: SPCK/Philadelphia: Westminster, 1978.

Boismard, M.-É. *Moses or Jesus: An Essay in Johannine Christology.* Translated by B. T. Viviano. Minneapolis: Fortress, 1993.

Borgen, P. *Bread from Heaven: An Exegetical Study of the Concept of Manna in the Gospel of John and the Writings of Philo.* Novum Testamentum Supplement 10. Leiden: Brill, 1965.

————. "Creation, Logos and the Son: Observations on John 1:1–18 and 5:17–18." *Ex Auditu* 3 (1987): 89–92.

————. *"Logos Was the True Light" and Other Essays on the Gospel of John.* Trondheim: Tapir, 1983.

————. *"Paul Preaches Circumcision and Pleases Men" and Other Essays on Christian Origins.* Trondheim: Tapir, 1983.

————. *Philo, John, and Paul: New Perspectives on Judaism and Early Christianity.* Atlanta: Scholars Press, 1987.

Brown, R. E. *The Birth of the Messiah: A Commentary on the Infancy Narratives in the Gospels of Matthew and Luke.* 2d edition. Anchor Bible Reference Library. New York: Doubleday, 1993.

————. *The Gospel according to John: Introduction, Translation, Notes.* 2 vols. Anchor Bible 29–29A. Garden City: Doubleday, 1966–70.

Bultmann, R. *The Gospel of John: A Commentary.* Translated by G. R. Beasley-Murray. Oxford: Blackwell, 1971.

Charlesworth, J. H. "The Jewish Roots of Christology: The Discovery of the Hypostatic Voice." *Scottish Journal of Theology* 39 (1986): 19–41.

———(ed.). *The Old Testament Pseudepigrapha.* 2 vols. New York: Doubleday, 1983–85.

Colson, F. H., and G. H. Whitaker (eds. and trans.). *Philo: With an English Translation.* 10 vols. Loeb Classical Library. Cambridge: Harvard University Press, 1929–62.

Coughenour, R. A. "The Wisdom Stance of Enoch's Redactor." *Journal for the Study of Judaism in the Persian, Hellenistic, and Roman Periods* 13 (1982): 47–55.

Crenshaw, J. L. *Old Testament Wisdom: An Introduction.* Atlanta: John Knox, 1981.

Culpepper, R. A., and C. C. Black (eds.). *Exploring the Gospel of John: In Honor of D. Moody Smith.* Louisville: Westminster John Knox, 1996.

Day, J., R. P. Gordon, and H. G. M. Williamson (eds.). *Wisdom in Ancient Israel: Essays in Honour of J. A. Emerton.* Cambridge: Cambridge University Press, 1995.

Deutsch, C. M. *Lady Wisdom, Jesus, and the Sages.* Valley Forge, Pa.: Trinity, 1996.

Dodd, C. H. *The Interpretation of the Fourth Gospel.* Cambridge: Cambridge University Press, 1953.

Eaton, J. *The Contemplative Face of Old Testament Wisdom in the Context of World Religions.* London: SCM/Philadelphia: Trinity, 1989.

Evans, C. A. *Word and Glory: On the Exegetical and Theological Background of John's Prologue.* Journal for the Study of the New Testament Supplement 89. Sheffield: Sheffield Academic Press, 1993.

Harrington, D. J. *Wisdom Texts from Qumran.* London/New York: Routledge, 1996.

Harris, J. R. *The Origin of the Prologue to St. John's Gospel.* Cambridge: Cambridge University Press, 1917.

Jonge, M. de (ed.). *L'Évangile de Jean.* Leuven: Leuven University Press, 1977.

Käsemann, E. *The Testament of Jesus according to John 17.* Translated by G. Krodel. Philadelphia: Fortress, 1968.

Loader, W. *The Christology of the Fourth Gospel: Structure and Issues.* Beiträge zur biblischen Exegese und Theologie 23. Berlin/New York: Lang, 1992.

Marcus, R. (trans.) *Philo: Questions and Answers on Genesis* and *Questions and Answers on Exodus*. 2 vols. Loeb Classical Library. Cambridge: Harvard University Press, 1953.

Martyn, J. L. *History and Theology in the Fourth Gospel*. 2d edition. Nashville: Abingdon, 1979.

Meeks, W. A. *The Prophet-King: Moses Traditions and the Johannine Christology*. Novum Testamentum Supplement 14. Leiden: Brill, 1967.

Moloney, F. J. *Glory Not Dishonor: Reading John 13–21*. Minneapolis: Fortress, 1998.

———. *The Johannine Son of Man*. 2d edition. Rome: LAS, 1978.

Murphy, R. E. *The Tree of Life: An Exploration of Biblical Wisdom Literature*. Anchor Bible Reference Library. New York: Doubleday, 1990.

Perdue, L. G. *Wisdom and Creation: The Theology of Wisdom Literature*. Nashville: Abingdon, 1994.

Rad, G. von. *Wisdom in Israel*. Translated by J. D. Martin. London: SCM/Nashville: Abingdon, 1972.

Ridderbos, H. *The Gospel of John*. Translated by J. Vriend. Grand Rapids: Eerdmans, 1997.

Schnackenburg, R. *The Gospel according to St. John*. 3 vols. Herder's Theological Commentary on the New Testament. New York: Crossroad, 1968–82.

Scott, M. *Sophia and the Johannine Jesus*. Journal for the Study of the New Testament Supplement 71. Sheffield: Sheffield Academic Press, 1992.

Scott, R. B. Y. *The Way of Wisdom in the Old Testament*. New York: Macmillan, 1971.

Smith, D. J. *The Theology of the Gospel of John*. Cambridge: Cambridge University Press, 1995.

Stibbe, M. W. G. *John*. Readings: A New Biblical Commentary. Sheffield: JSOT Press, 1993.

Stone, M. E. (ed.). *Jewish Writings of the Second Temple Period: Apocrypha, Pseudepigrapha, Qumran Sectarian Writings, Philo, Josephus*. Compendia rerum iudaicarum ad Novum Testamentum 2.2. Assen: Van Gorcum/Philadelphia: Fortress, 1984.

Willett, M. E. *Wisdom Christology in the Fourth Gospel*. San Francisco: Mellen, 1992.

Winston, D. *Philo of Alexandria*. New York: Paulist, 1981.

Witherington, B., III. *Jesus the Sage: The Pilgrimage of Wisdom*. Minneapolis: Fortress, 1994.

———. *John's Wisdom: A Commentary on the Fourth Gospel*. Louisville: Westminster/John Knox, 1995.

Index of Ancient Sources

Index of Modern Authors